THE HEARTS
OF MEN

THE HEARTS OF MEN

American Dreams and the Flight from Commitment

Barbara Ehrenreich

ANCHOR BOOKS
DOUBLEDAY
NEW YORK LONDON TORONTO SYDNEY AUCKLAND

AN ANCHOR BOOK
PUBLISHED BY DOUBLEDAY
a division of Bantam Doubleday Dell Publishing Group, Inc.
666 Fifth Avenue, New York, New York 10103

ANCHOR BOOKS, DOUBLEDAY, and the portrayal of an anchor
are trademarks of Doubleday, a division of Bantam Doubleday
Dell Publishing Group, Inc.

The Hearts of Men was originally published in hardcover
by Anchor Books/Doubleday in 1983.

Library of Congress Cataloging-in-Publication Data
Ehrenreich, Barbara.
 The hearts of men.
 Includes index.
  1. Men—Psychology. 2. Sex role. 3. Marriage.
I. Title.
HQ1090.E36 1983   305.3'1   82 45104
ISBN 0-385-17615-5

ACKNOWLEDGMENTS

This book was made possible by a Ford Foundation Award for Humanistic Perspectives on Contemporary Society and by a fellowship from the New York Institute for the Humanities. I thank the latter institution not only for financial support, but for the collegial environment it has provided me for the past two years.

At the beginning of this project I often feared that I was straying too far from the conventional—and, indeed, even feminist—wisdom about what has happened between men and women in the past couple of decades. Fortunately, a number of thoughtful people urged me to persist—Richard Sennett, Marilyn Young, Frances Fox Piven, Ann Fergusen and Deirdre English—and I thank them for their questions as well as their confidence in me. Along the way, Howard Gadlin, Joel Kovel, Joe Interrante and Jane O'Reilly took the time to help clear up some particularly baffling points and to suggest additional sources. Several friends were enlisted to read and comment on particular chapters: Peter Biskind, John Ehrenreich, Elizabeth Hess and Bob Fitch. I am especially thankful to Bill Leach, who read the entire manuscript in, more or less, one sitting, and to Patrick Merla, who did most of the typing. Both of them offered useful suggestions of both an editorial and substantive nature. Finally, I have had the good fortune to work once again with Loretta Barrett at Doubleday, who is not only an insightful and energetic editor, but a good friend. Needless to say, I sometimes ignored all these people's advice, and that should account for any errors or lapses of judgment in what follows.

I would also like to thank Nancy Boensch for her contribution to the typing and her unfailing good humor. The librarians of the Nassau County Library System are to be commended for their courteous helpfulness in the face of many peculiar requests. Credit is also due to Rosa Ehrenreich and Benjamin Ehrenreich for providing refreshing distractions as well as loving support.

This book is dedicated to those people who came through when I needed them—Diane Alexander, Deirdre English, Elizabeth Hess, Gloria Jacobs, Barbara Riddle and Ruth Russell— and to the vision of community which they have helped keep alive for me.

CONTENTS

THE HEARTS
OF MEN

1

INTRODUCTION

Why Women Married Men

Necessity, as well as instinct, sends the ladies pell-
mell to the altar; it is only the secondary things,
social pressure or conscience, that send the men.
—Emily Hahn, 1956

The fact that men marry in precisely the same numbers as
women do conceals a basic inequality of motivation: namely,
that in the sort of marriage we have rather suddenly come to
see as "traditional," women need men much more than men
need women. When I was growing up in the fifties, everyone
acknowledged the "battle of the sexes" in which women "held
out" for as long as possible, until, by dint of persuasion, sexual
frustration or sudden pregnancy, they "landed a man." From
their side of the battle lines, men viewed the proceedings with
a certain sarcastic detachment. For example, a 1958 article in
Esquire described courtship with humorous references to the
military theories of Field Marshal Rommel and offered the
following account of a typical girl's attempt to win an "MRS"
degree:

> College is four years, okay? . . . A freshman dates every-
> body. She doesn't care. A sophomore dates in flurries.
> . . . Now a junior is looking for real love. She'll go out
> three times with a boy who is a Possible. She may worry:
> there aren't enough Possibles in her immediate circle of
> friends. So she gets interested in extra-curricular activities,

French club, things like that. . . . Finally there are senior
girls. If they aren't going steady or engaged by November
first, they feel the walls closing in. They date only Proba-
bles. . . . They talk about a career, but they don't mean
it. Let them have six dates with one boy—they'll have him
talking about compatibility and the names of their five
children.[1]

To a young woman of spirit, the battle of the sexes seemed
to be a degrading exercise that was hardly worth the prize.
From what I could tell of my mother's life, "victory" meant a
life sentence to manual labor, relieved only by the intellectual
challenge of family quarrels. Yet the grown men around me
were, if anything, even more prone to bitterness, and fond of
declaiming on the theme of marriage as a "trap" for men and a
lifelong sinecure for women. Throughout my childhood I was
mystified as to what forces propelled people—especially women
—into the "battle" of courtship and, beyond that, the prolonged hostilities of wedded life.

The answer, when it was finally revealed to me later in life,
had as much to do with economics as biology. Women were,
and to a large extent still are, economically dependent on men.
After all, a man could live on his own. He might be lonely,
unkempt and nostalgic for home-cooked food, but he would,
more than likely, get by. A woman, on the other hand, would
be hard pressed to make a living on her own at all. If she had
spent her college years changing majors in pursuit of "Proba-
bles," or her married life changing diapers, so much the worse;
she could expect to enter the labor market as a saleswoman or
a waitress earning something near the minimum wage. So what
was at stake for women in the battle of the sexes was, crudely
put, a claim on some man's wage. Both sexes, of course, were
under intense social pressure to enter the fray and resolve it by
"settling down," but the penalities for failure were very different. The man who failed to marry or stay married might be
judged a little "odd"; the woman might well be poor. In the
eyes of the middle-class, mid-century world, he had dodged a
responsibility, while she had missed the boat.

The fact that, in a purely economic sense, women need men

more than the other way round, gives marriage an inherent instability that predates the sexual revolution, the revival of feminism, the "me generation" or other well-worn explanations for what has come to be known as the "breakdown of the family." It is, in retrospect, frightening to think how much of our sense of social order and continuity has depended on the willingness of men to succumb in the battle of the sexes: to marry, to become wage earners and to reliably share their wages with their dependents. In fact, most of us require more comforting alternative descriptions of the bond between men and women. We romanticize it, as in the popular song lyrics of the fifties where love was an adventure culminating either in matrimony or premature death. Or we convince ourselves that there is really a fair and equal exchange at work so that the wages men offer to women are more than compensated for by the services women offer to men. Any other conclusion would be a grave embarrassment to both sexes. Women do not like to admit to a disproportionate dependence, just as men do not like to admit that they may have been conned into undertaking what one cynical male called "the lifelong support of the female unemployed."

Social scientists have generally shared these aversions and, on the whole, their accounts of the economics of marriage tend to be flustered or nonexistent. In the early to mid-1970s sociologists produced no less than a half dozen anthologies on the family—its future, its prospects, its changing forms—but few gave more than a passing acknowledgment to its principal source of livelihood—the male wage—and the consequences of that dependence for both internal family relations and the relations of larger social groups.* To judge from much of this literature, marriage exists in some realm outside of ordinary economic ties, and families operate more or less like voluntary

---

* In one of the rare exceptions within this genre of "family" books Louise Kapp Howe observed trenchantly that ". . . the assumption of a male-breadwinner society—and the social policies and occupational structure and sexist attitudes that flow from that assumption—ends up determining the lives of everyone within a family, whether a male breadwinner is present or not, whether one is living by the rules in suburbia trying to break them on a commune."[2]

associations or social clubs, which the members have opted to join.

The intellectual groundwork for such an innocent view of marriage had been laid by early twentieth-century social scientists, foremost among them the historian Arthur W. Calhoun. Calhoun was enthusiastic about the modern family he saw emerging from the wilderness past. The old-style, agrarian family had been a unit of production, its members bound together, somewhat brutishly, by economic necessity. Then came industrialization and the removal of production (cloth and clothing manufacture, food processing, etc.) from the home. The modern family, freed from the imperative of collective work, was thought to be no longer bound by economic necessity, but by more "spiritual" needs and concerns. At a safe remove from the commercial world outside, the family "ceases to be a forced grouping, and develops toward ethical unity and spontaneous democracy." To Calhoun and the scholars who followed him, the "companionate family," insulated from the competitiveness and commercialism of the "economy" outside, was not just a liberal ideal, but a description of reality.

What was missing, in this description, was the economy of the family itself. On this point, even Calhoun sometimes wavered. He had thrown "economic necessity" out of the family with the coming of the industrial revolution, and was far too chivalrous to admit that it might be a new kind of economic necessity that bound the modern woman to her husband. Yet when he looked at the middle-class families of his time, he found disturbing signs. Too many women had become "parasitic wives." Too many men had been reduced to mere "earning mechanisms." It occurred to him that with industrialization and the removal of women's traditional productive work from the home, "the father comes to view the family as a responsibility rather than an asset." Grimly, he suggested that this might be "part of the explanation for the phenomenon of family desertion [by men]."[3]

While Calhoun was equivocating, two of his contemporaries were taking a more hard-headed look at the economics of marriage and the family. They were both intellectual mavericks: one a feminist and a socialist, the other a conservative and a self-professed misogynist. If only because of the tenacity of more sentimental views, their ideas are still fresh, and even radical, today.

Charlotte Perkins Gilman, the feminist writer and lecturer, came to her views on marriage from unhappy personal experience. Her father was one of the deserters Calhoun warned about. He walked out when Charlotte was very young, leaving his erstwhile family in poverty. Her own marriage to a young painter looked more promising, for, as she later wrote, "a lover more tender, a husband more devoted, woman could not ask." But shortly after the birth of their child, Charlotte (then Stetson) developed a protracted case of what was then called nervous prostration and what we now diagnose as depression. During the ensuing months of prostration and "absolute misery" she had time to contemplate the dark side of even the best marriage. Divorced and largely recovered, she undertook a strenuous, lifelong assault on those things most of her suffragist contemporaries claimed to hold even dearer than the vote—the traditional middle-class marriage and family.

Gilman described the economics of marriage in the language of biology, and the effect was brutal: "The female of the genus homo is economically dependent on the male," she wrote. "He is her food supply."[4] Marriage was a "sexuo-economic relation," in which men paid money for the personal services performed by women, and paid, ironically, in inverse relation to the work performed. The wives of the poor, lacking servants and conveniences, had to work the hardest and were paid the least: "The women who do the most work get the least money, and the women who get the most money do the least work." Within the middle and upper classes, women's position was parasitical. Most of the tasks they performed could either be done by men and children themselves, abolished without any great discomfort, or (in her utopian vision) collectivized through the creation of inexpensive cafeterias, laundromats, day-care centers, etc. With the domestic work thus dispersed or dispensed with, women would be free to enter the work force as independent wage earners and to enter marriage as men's equals.

Within the prevailing "sexuo-economic" system, men got the best deal, Gilman thought—though only in moral terms. True, men had to pay a high price for dubious and often inept domestic services, but this was good for them. Anticipating Betty Friedan, she believed that dependency and exclusive concentration on domestic detail infantilized women, potentially making them unfit even for the central vocation of motherhood. And, anticipating George Gilder, she believed that the role of the provider uplifted and "maternalized" men, taming "the destructive action of male energy" and teaching men "to love and care, to work, to serve, to be human." The question Gilman left open was why men should voluntarily undertake such a costly and demanding course in self-improvement.

The iconoclastic journalist H. L. Mencken had an answer, though it is doubtful that Gilman would have liked it. If men got married, he wrote, it was because they were stupid. In a 1918 book cunningly entitled *In Defense of Women,* he described the average man as "an almost incredible popinjay," easily duped by the scheming female of the species. Pathetically, the average male "views it as a great testimony to his prowess at amour to yield up his liberty, his property and his soul to the first woman who, in despair of finding better game, turns her appraising eye upon him." Once married, a man's legal status was little better than an indentured servant's, for "under the contract of marriage, all the duties lie upon the man and all the privileges appertain to the woman." The law required a man to support his wife, but it did not require her to so much as prepare a decent meal, so that

> If the average American husband wants a sound dinner he must go to a restaurant to get it, just as if he wants to refresh himself with the society of charming and well-behaved children, he has to go to an orphan asylum.[5]

Whether the average husband sought his meals at diners, his female company at dance halls and his paternal satisfactions among street urchins, he would still be supporting his own wife and children. And if this seems like a somewhat overwrought description of the male condition, the reader should know that Mencken's intellectual credentials were in perfect order: He himself was a bachelor. Bachelorhood proved a man's "relative freedom from the ordinary sentimentalism of his sex—in other words, of his greater approximation to the clearheadedness of the enemy sex."

Each in their own way, the misogynist Mencken and the feminist Gilman saw through the romance of marriage to the economic reality: In modern industrial society, which was supposed to have freed personal relationships from the bonds of economic necessity, women were the dependents of men. What even Gilman did not fully grasp was that this dependency had become embedded in the workings of the larger economy, and that it would persist—despite the efforts of women and the protests of an occasional male dissident like Mencken—right through the middle of the century.

The American economy, by the early twentieth century, was based on the principle of the family wage: A male worker should be paid enough to support a family. I say "principle" to distinguish from reality. The reality through most of this century is that only the more privileged male workers—those who are members of powerful unions, or of skilled crafts and professions—actually earned enough to support a family. Yet the principle, as Louise Kapp Howe observes, applied to everyone: as a goal for personal upward mobility (a man took pride in the fact that his wife didn't "have" to work) and as a social ideal. Socialists advocated the family wage, trade unionists fought for it, and most feminists, by the turn of the century, either approved or did not oppose it. But, as historian Heidi Hartmann has explained, the fight for the family wage helped establish our present gender-based occupational hierarchy.[6] Women were squeezed out of higher paying, craft jobs and professions and pushed down to the bottom of the labor market. As it turned out, the other side of the principle that a man should earn enough to support a family has been that a woman doesn't need enough to support even herself.

The perpetuation of the family wage system has depended on two things, one a fact, the other an assumption. The fact is that men, on the average, earn more than women. The assumption is that men use their higher wages to support women, and hence that most women are at least partly supported by men. It is easy to see how the assumption has reinforced the fact, and vice versa. If it is assumed that most women are already supported by men, then they can, in good conscience, be paid less than men. And if women cannot expect to earn a decent wage on their own, they will indeed seek the financial support of individual men. Which reinforces the assumption that men, as supporters of women, deserve higher wages than women, and so forth.

Hence, the basic asymmetry of need that shaped what we used to call "battle of the sexes." The family wage system guarantees that, at least for economic reasons, women will have a greater interest in marrying and in marrying "well," and a greater financial stake in their marriages than men do. Within this unequal situation, the one thing that salvages women's dignity is the fact that they "work" too, even when not employed outside the home. But domestic labor, Charlotte Perkins Gilman pointed out, has an awkward and uncertain status. Those of us who do it, and I write from personal experience, know that the work of raising children and maintaining a home is mentally demanding, physically strenuous and almost wholly unappreciated by fellow adults. Yet we also know that, above some irreducible biological minimum at which children will go hungry and guests will contract infectious diseases from our dishware, we work at our own pace and according to our own standards. These standards are personal and variable. They are also, as Deirdre English and I argued in *For Her Own Good,* determined by the "expert" arbiters of what constitutes good housekeeping and adequate mothering.[7] So we ourselves are often hard pressed to tell how much of our work we do out of conformity—or, in some cases, compulsiveness—and how much out of necessity. And whatever we do, we know that men, at least, can survive without it. As sociologist Carol Brown has written:

A wife's personal labor can now be replaced by commercial products, such as self-cleaning ovens. The labor of women is available outside the home. Waitresses serve food and clean tables; nurses tend sick bodies; therapists provide shoulders to cry on. Third, women are publicly available, giving service with a smile on their jobs or sex with a smile after hours. Thus men do not have the incentive to find and cleave unto just one woman until death do they part.[8]

In their official capacities, men have tended to extoll the work of homemaking and child raising, but they seldom offer to pay for it with public funds. President Theodore Roosevelt, for example, once declared homemaking a "career . . . more worthy of honor and . . . more useful to the community than the career of any man, no matter how successful."[9] Yet neither he nor any of his successors offered women any financial recognition for their efforts, and what public relief became available with the New Deal fell miserably short of the income by which a man would have been judged "successful." Whether homemaking is an essential career, as Roosevelt claimed, or merely a "pseudo-occupation," as sociologist Talcott Parsons later concluded, it has been left to the sponsorship of individual men.

So, well before the recent alarm about the "breakdown of the family," the twentieth-century family wage system had the makings of serious instability. The problems, a modern social scientist might say, were "structural," that is, they were always there, embedded in the very design of the system. If we accept the formulation of the anthropologist Claude Levi-Strauss, the heterosexual bond depends on a firm division of labor; A woman does X (which could be weaving cloth, tending a store or raising heirs) and a man does Y (which could be fishing or herding or accounting). The only rules are (1) that X be rigidly typed as a female activity and Y as a male activity, so that no one person would be able to do both X and Y for themselves, and (2) that X be considered a pretty fair exchange for Y. But in industrial capitalist societies, the female X became a set of activities which men could do and often did do for themselves (with the single clear-cut exception of bearing babies) and the male Y boiled down to the business of earning a living. Moreover, the X that women have normally been confined to was an occupation of dubious status and limited marketability. Any man who achieved what Mencken described as "the clearheadedness of the enemy sex" could reasonably conclude that the exchange of Y for X was a poor bargain.

The reader may object that this is far too cold-hearted an analysis. There is, after all, love; there is sexual desire; and there is a kind of emotional dependency that can outlast sexual enthusiasm for decades. In her book *The Future of Marriage*, Jessie Bernard argues that when the intangible satisfactions of marriage are taken into account, it is men, and not women, who are disproportionately dependent. Married men live longer than their single counterparts, and, according to surveys, are happier and more likely to be judged mentally healthy. Among women, there is evidence that the opposite is true; full-time housewives, at any rate, are "sicker" than other women by a variety of measures. Bernard acknowledges that "marriage has had a bad press among men," but insists that "whether they know it or not, men need marriage more than women do." She even speculates that male resentment of marriage represents "a kind of compensatory reaction to their dependence on it."[10]

Bernard may be right about men's dependence on the loving care of women. But when we put money back into the exchange, the old asymmetry reappears. In a traditional marriage —that is, the union of a male breadwinner and a female homemaker—the husband may need a variety of emotional satisfactions, as may the wife. But the wife needs, in addition, the wherewithal to buy the groceries, and there is no guarantee that a man's emotional dependency on his wife will last as long as her financial dependency on him. The family wage system takes no account of that great truth reiterated endlessly on AM radio stations: that love is fickle.

The law acknowledges women's financial dependency and, at least in principle, adjures married men to share their wages. In her comprehensive book *The Marriage Contract,* Lenore Weitzman reports that almost every state places legal responsibility on the husband to support his wife and children. For example, a 1973 Pennsylvania court stated that "the husband has an absolute moral and legal obligation to support his wife . . ." But, as Weitzman explains, neither the extent of this "obligation" nor the level of support in relation to a man's income has ever been defined, so that the "right to support" in practice means little more than "the privilege of living with the husband."[11] After divorce, the law takes only slightly more interest in a woman's financial situation: Only 25 percent of the women who are awarded child support by the courts actually receive it, and 60 percent of these receive less than $1,500 a year.[12] In short, though a man may earn a "family wage," there is nothing in the law that compels him to share it.

This is perhaps the greatest weakness in any social system based on the principle of the family wage: It depends so much on the volition of individual men. Men are favored in the labor market, both by the kinds of occupations open to them and by informal discrimination within occupations, so that they earn, on the average, 40 percent more than women do. Yet nothing compels them to spread the wealth to those—women and children—who are excluded from work or less generously rewarded for it. Men cannot be forced to marry; once married, they cannot be forced to bring home their paychecks, to be reliable jobholders or, of course, to remain married. In fact, considering the absence of legal coercion, the surprising thing is that men have for so long, and, on the whole, so reliably, adhered to what we might call the "breadwinner ethic."

* * *

This book is about the ideology that shaped the breadwinner ethic and how that ideology collapsed, as a persuasive set of expectations, in just the last thirty years. To describe the change very briefly and oversimply: In the 1950s, where we begin, there was a firm expectation (or as we would now say, "role") that required men to grow up, marry and support their wives. To do anything else was less than grown-up, and the man who willfully deviated was judged to be somehow "less than a man." This expectation was supported by an enormous weight of expert opinion, moral sentiment and public bias, both within popular culture and the elite centers of academic wisdom. But by the end of the 1970s and the beginning of the 1980s, adult manhood was no longer burdened with the automatic expectation of marriage and breadwinning. The man who postpones marriage even into middle age, who avoids women who are likely to become financial dependents, who is dedicated to his own pleasures, is likely to be found not suspiciously deviant, but "healthy." And this judgment, like the prior one, is supported by expert opinion and by the moral sentiments and biases of a considerable sector of the American middle class.

This drastic change in our cultural expectations of men has been ignored, down-played or else buried under the weary rubric of "changing sex roles." Obviously, our expectations of adult womanhood have changed just as dramatically in the last thirty years. The old feminine ideal—the full-time housewife with a station wagon full of children—has been largely replaced by the career woman with attaché case and skirted suit. Partly because the changes in women's role have been given conscious articulation by a feminist movement, changes in men (or in the behavior expected of men) are usually believed to be derivative of, or merely reactive to, the changes in women. Yet I will argue that the collapse of the breadwinner ethic had begun well before the revival of feminism and stemmed from dissatisfactions every bit as deep, if not as idealistically expressed, as those that motivated our founding "second wave" feminists.

Further, I will want to impress on you the profundity of the change represented by the collapse of the breadwinner ethic. In the space of a few decades, our culture has inverted the expectations that made the family wage system in any sense justifiable as a means of distributing wealth from those who are relatively advantaged as wage earners to many of those (women and children) who are not. Men still have the incentives to work and even to succeed at dreary and manifestly useless jobs, but not necessarily to work for others.

This is a book about ideas, images, perceptions, opinions

from various sources—and I leave it to the sociologists to trace the behavioral and attitudinal changes that have accompanied the changes in ideas. But ideas do come from someone, and in our society, the ideas we live by and shape our judgments in accordance with, have tended to come from the men (and, more rarely, women) of what is variously called the "new class," the "professional-managerial class" or far less precisely, the middle class. This is not to discount the generative role of the capitalist class, which employs so much of the professional-managerial middle class, or of the working class, which is, in turn, educated, managed and often even spoken for by the middle class. But in a year-by-year sense it is the men in the middle who are the "knowledge producers," whether they are generating "scientific" truths about human nature and possibilities, distilling these truths for popular consumption, or reflecting upon them in fiction and films. These men crafted and popularized the ideology that had supported the breadwinner ethic, and when the ideology changed, it was because *they* changed it. For this reason I feel justified in using a more active construction than the "collapse of the breadwinner ethic" and talking about a *male revolt*—though hardly organized and seldom conscious of its goals—against the breadwinner ethic.

As a feminist, I have been busy with another revolt for the past twelve years, and I approached this one with initial antagonism, a gradual increase in understanding and, finally, a certain impatience. The great irony, as I will argue later, is that the right-wing, antifeminist backlash that emerged in the 1970s is a backlash not so much against feminism as against the male revolt. We live in a time that is dangerous to dissidents of all persuasions, and not least to those too helpless and impoverished to dissent. The question is whether we rebels of both sexes have enough in common to work together toward a more generous, dignified and caring society.

2

BREADWINNERS AND
LOSERS

Sanctions Against Male Deviance

> A young college-educated bourgeois male of my generation who scoffed at the idea of marriage for himself, who would just as soon eat out of cans or in cafeterias, sweep his own floor, make his own bed, and come and go with no binding legal attachments . . . laid himself open to the charge of "immaturity," if not "latent" or blatant "homosexuality." Or he was just plain "selfish." Or was "frightened of responsibility." Or he could not "commit himself" (nice institutional phrase, that) to a "permanent relationship."
>
> –Philip Roth, *My Life as a Man*, 1974

Few men would admit to marrying for reasons other than love or domestic incompetence. Yet as late as 1966, a leading American psychoanalyst and writer, Dr. Hendrik Ruitenbeek, observed that

> Contemporary America seems to have no room for the mature bachelor. As a colleague of mine once remarked, a single man over thirty is now regarded as a pervert, a person with severe emotional problems, or a poor creature fettered to mother.[1]

The average age of marriage for men in the late fifties was twenty-three, and according to popular wisdom, if a man held out much longer, say even to twenty-seven, "you had to wonder." Psychiatrists like Dr. Ruitenbeek and his colleagues were hardly aloof from the popular prejudice against "overaged," unmarried men, however. By the 1950s and '60s psychiatry had developed a massive weight of theory establishing that marriage—and, within that, the breadwinner role—was the only normal state for the adult male. Outside lay only a range of diagnoses, all unflattering.

On the face of it, the construction of a scientific justification for the male breadwinner role was a somewhat more challenging enterprise than explaining why little girls necessarily grew up to be wives and mothers. For women, biology was more clearly destiny, and Freudians had no trouble navigating the developmental passage from the first menses to baby showers and PTA membership. It was more difficult to trace how the possession of a penis should lead its owner into a middle-management career and Little League weekends. This was the task that psychoanalyst Therese Benedek set for herself in her study of "Fatherhood and Providing," an effort that illustrates, if nothing else, the deep faith her profession has had in the "naturalness" of the male breadwinner role.

Benedek's hypothesis was that the conventional male role, like that of the female, has "instinctual roots." With women, things were straightforward, since "mothering behavior is regulated by a pituitary hormone." In the case of men, no fathering/providing hormone was, as yet, "recognizable" so she cited the exemplary behavior of male birds and certain species of fish, who, unlike most male mammals, show a nurturant interest in their young. Undeterred by the phylogenetic gap between robins and humans, she stated that

> These observations prove that providing food and security is not a culturally imposed burden on the male of the species but "nature's order."

Furthermore, providing was linked to the male's "instinctual drive for survival," and the evidence for this was that men prefer male children; i.e., children who seem to be extensions of themselves. Whether father robins also prefer baby males, or whether human males might feel a lesser urge to provide for their little girls, was not investigated. As if sensing the socio-biological quagmire she had opened up, Benedek made a final appeal to history. "All significant cultures," she wrote, "have developed on the basis that the husband-father is the chief protector and provider of the family." Over time, this arrangement had been so thoroughly imprinted that instincts were not really necessary after all:

> Repeated through countless generations, transferred from fathers to sons, man's role as provider has become independent of its biologic roots.

But neither these ingrained habits nor the avian instincts were 100 percent reliable, and, in describing the male "failures" Benedek unwittingly opened the door to a more voluntaristic account of male behavior. "We know men often avoid marriage and parenthood," she wrote. "There are fathers who abandon wife and child; often such men become 'bums' (vagabonds) . . ." drifting out of sight in order to "avoid civilization." But she did not ascribe their failure—as her own theory would have required—to an insufficient nesting instinct or the heritage of an "insignificant" culture or similar accident of fate. Men who rejected the provider role were, in her final judgment, simply "afraid of the responsibilities involved."[2]

Most psychologists and psychoanalysts rejected biology in favor of a less deterministic and more strenuous account of man's ascent to the breadwinner role. In the 1950s Erik Erikson had introduced the idea of the "life cycle," punctuated by crises and culminating, if all went well, in a state of maturity. This was a departure from Freud, who had concentrated all the critical psychological dramas in the preschool years (a choice that, incidentally, was important in reinforcing the need for full-time mothering until a woman's youngest child was at least six years old). After that there was nothing left but to work out, or repeat, the patterns laid down in the toddler years. Erikson not only extended the psychoanalytically interesting life span, but introduced new elements of responsibility and choice. A person could perform the developmental "tasks" required to move from one stage of the life cycle to the next, or he or she could get stuck and fail to advance toward maturity. Nowhere did Erikson specify the precise content of the various stages of occupational terms (though his scheme bears a certain resemblance to the career trajectory of a successful college professor). But "maturity" and the "tasks" which led to it quickly entered the psychologists' vocabulary as professional code words for conformity.

It is difficult, in the wake of the sixties' youth rebellion, to appreciate the weight and authority that once attached to the word "maturity." Looking back on his first marriage in the 1950s, A. Alvarez wrote in 1981, "I had this terrible lust for premature maturity, this irresponsible desire for responsibility, before I had any idea what maturity involved or had ever tasted the pleasures of youthful irresponsibility."[3] Maturity was not dull, but "heroic," a measured acceptance of the limits of one's private endeavors at a time when action on a broader political scale could only seem foolish—or suspect. Novels like *The Man in the Gray Flannel Suit* and *Marjorie Morningstar* endorsed maturity, and the 1950 best seller *The Mature Mind* held it up as an evolutionary achievement.

In the opening pages of *The Mature Mind,* author H. A. Overstreet describes all scientific endeavor—physics, chemistry, biology and psychology—as preliminary gropings toward "the maturity concept." At last, "its full meaning begins to dawn on us . . . this is what our past wisdoms have been leading up to." And none too soon, for in Overstreet's view, every possible human folly can be chalked up to "immaturity"—war, racism, labor unrest, social injustice, promiscuity and even the annoying tendency of some people to play practical jokes. "Jesus Christ," Overstreet wrote approvingly, "is reported to have said one of the maturest things ever said by a suffering human being," for in asking forgiveness for his crucifiers, he recognized that they were "not bad," only immature.

Maturity itself required the predictable, sober ingredients of wisdom, responsibility, empathy, (mature) heterosexuality and "a sense of function," or, as a sociologist would have put it, acceptance of adult sex roles. Thus, a woman would be immature "if she wants all the advantages of marriage" but resents doing housework, and a man would be less-than-grown-up if he shirked the breadwinner role:

> . . . a man is immature if he regards the support of a family as a kind of trap in which he, an unsuspecting male, has somehow been caught. Again, the person who cannot settle down, who remains a vocational drifter, or the person who wants the prestige of a certain type of work but resents the routines that go with it, are immature in their sense of function.[4]

How did a man attain maturity? In 1953 the psychologist R. J. Havighurst discovered eight "developmental tasks of early adulthood," the performance of which was a prerequisite for mature adulthood. The list, which was to be repeated in developmental psychology textbooks for nearly three decades, included: (1) selecting a mate, (2) learning to live with a marriage partner, (3) starting a family, (4) rearing children, (5) managing a home, (6) getting started in an occupation, (7) taking on civic responsibilities and (8) finding a congenial social group. In the developmental psychology literature of the 1950s, it would not take too much supplementary reading to figure out that tasks 4 and 5 are the special responsibility of the female marriage partner, and that 6 was the special province of the male.

The fact that the developmental tasks "discovered" by psychologists so closely paralleled the expectations one might find in the *Reader's Digest* seemed only to enhance their scientific status. One textbook in developmental psychology reassures the student that the tasks about to be listed will be no surprise, since "social expectations for the young adult in our culture are clearly defined and familiar to him even before he reaches legal maturity."[5] Another introduces the checklist with the irrefutable observation that "maturity is contingent upon the number of adult developmental tasks successfully completed."[6] Others—and these are texts still widely read by social work students and others in the helping professions—offered more detailed psychological insights into challenges of adult life, such as: "The prompt payment of bills demands a degree of perspective and maturity."[7]

Marriage was not only a proof of maturity, it was a chance to exercise one's maturity through countless new "tasks." Men as well as women were to build a "working partnership," overcome romance for "a realistic conception of marriage" and seek a mutual state of "emotional maturity." Even love required discipline and maturity. "Love in marriage has to be worked at," counseled a 1962 marriage manual. "Both the giving part and the receiving part have to be worked at. The last part may sound strange because we ordinarily think that the receiving part will take care of itself. It doesn't though, any more than the giving part."[8]

In the novel *When She Was Good,* Philip Roth satirized the approved male attitude toward marriage-as-work in a passage that could almost have been lifted from a text on personality development. Young Roy Bassart has given up his education and taken a job he despises in order to support Lucy and the baby. He would like nothing better than to run back to the comforts of his parents' home. But this is the early fifties, and Roy aspires to "be a man":

> The more he thought about it the more he realized that marriage was probably the most serious thing you did in your whole life . . . Instead of running off to Reno, Nevada, two people who have any maturity stop being kids, buckle down and really decide to *work* at marriage. Because that's the key word—work—which you don't know, of course, when you go waltzing into holy matrimony, thinking it is going to be a continuation of your easy-going pre-marital good times. No, marriage is work, and hard work, too . . .[9]

Outside of their marital endeavors, men had the ongoing opportunity to demonstrate their maturity by actually working at a paid job. This is what grown men did and what social scientists and psychologists, in turn, observed them doing. "It is perhaps not too much to say," Talcott Parsons said with all the caution of a scientist who is about to reveal a startling new observation about the natural world, "that only in very exceptional cases can an adult man be genuinely self-respecting and enjoy a respected status in the eyes of others if he does not 'earn a living' in an approved occupational role."[10] If the obligatory combination of marriage and job added up to a less-than-heroic definition of manhood, there were compensations. A 1959 text entitled *Psychology of Personal and Social Adjustment* offers a full-page picture of a man kneeling by the side of a pond with a toy boat. The caption says: "Building model ships is one of the numerous ways of finding outlets for creative needs."[11] Evidently, the quiet pond that lay at the end of the adult male developmental path was not Walden.

If adult masculinity was indistinguishable from the breadwinner role, then it followed that the man who failed to achieve this role was either not fully adult or not fully masculine. In the schema of male pathology developed by mid-century psychologists, immaturity shaded into infantilism, which was, in turn, a manifestation of unnatural fixation on the mother, and the entire complex of symptomatology reached its clinical climax in the diagnosis of homosexuality. Empirical findings were offered to support these judgments. In 1955 sociologist Manfred Kuhn reported eleven reasons for people's failure to marry. Some were simply misfortunes, such as "poor health or deviant physical characteristics," "unattractiveness" and extreme geographical isolation. But high on the list for men were homosexuality, emotion fixation on parent(s) and "unwillingness to assume responsibility."[12] Dr. Paul Popenoe, whose suspenseful case studies entitled "Can This Marriage Be Saved?" appeared regularly in the *Ladies' Home Journal*, blamed bachelorhood on "emotional immaturity and infantile fixations." He reported that studies at his American Institute for Family Relations "bear out the popular opinion that a mother-fixation is responsible for the celibacy of many old bachelors who might otherwise have been superior husbands." This was not as unfortunate as it may have seemed, for Dr. Popenoe's opinion of one of the most common varieties of "old" unmarried women, divorcées, was even lower than his opinion of the available men: These women, he wrote, "are to some extent biological inferiors and discards who do not offer good matrimonial prospects."[13]

In practice, psychiatrists could be as punitive toward the "immature" male as they were toward the recalcitrant female. Even small infractions could be evidence of serious disorders. In a chapter on "Adulthood" in a 1975 textbook for social workers, psychoanalyst Dr. Richard Burnett tells us that in the long ascent to maturity

> Sometimes there is a prolonged stalemate between progressive and regressive forces, and . . . pathological outcomes are frequent . . . Familiar examples are those who are unable to choose a mate or a vocation, finish college or a Ph.D. thesis.[14]

In case the gender is unclear here, we find on reading further that women should avoid the "narcissistic pursuit of career ambitions," which only takes them "further from feminine fulfillment along the route of masculinization." The overly striving woman was "poorly integrated and of persisting bisexual disposition," while a young man could presumably raise psychoanalytic suspicions by merely failing to complete a term paper.

Clinicians' reactions to men who actually cracked under the strain of breadwinning were, predictably, unsympathetic. The period immediately after the birth of a baby was especially likely to precipitate infantile and/or homosexual behavior in men who had only superficially accepted their responsibilities as breadwinners. A 1966 paper in the *American Journal of Psychiatry* presents ten case histories of men who required hospitalization for their post-partum breakdowns.[15] The case of a twenty-nine-year-old securities analyst is presented as an illustration of how financial responsibility can be "the initial precipitant of a psychoneurotic illness, with latent homosexual features playing an important dynamic role." During his wife's pregnancy he had "expressed some doubts about the added financial burden," and

> In a group of company executives he began to experience periodic anxiety attacks characterized by tachycardia, apprehension, marked perspiration, and anal paresthesias. He

functioned well, however, until his wife gave birth to a
son. He then became preoccupied with rapidly falling quo-
tations on a recent stock purchase and considered killing
his wife and himself.

The possibility that he hated his job and harbored inadmissible feelings toward the company executives, rather than his
baby, was not explored.

In another case, a twenty-nine-year-old mathematician, who
had long been anxious about his job, collapsed after the birth
of his fourth child, and was coldly labeled a "paranoid schizo-
phreniac." Others of the unfortunate fathers studied were described as "acting out"—spending money foolishly, having
affairs, drinking to excess, claiming to have developed an incurable disease or other forms of infantile and dependent behavior.

The occasional patient who found more articulate, less destructive ways to express his rebellion was not so easily labeled
as "infantile." At least, not quite so easily. In a case from the
above study, which is also featured in a major text on *Personality Development and Deviation,* we find a young scientist,
who, whenever the subject of parenthood came up

> . . . brought up his ardent wish for a racing car, which he
> did not need and could not afford. He brought it up each
> time his wife pleaded for a pregnancy. He gradually
> agreed that he would like to have a son, but that he would
> antagonize his Greek Orthodox parents by not baptizing
> his son and by naming him Darwin.[16]

Could this clear break from his own parents be taken as a sign
of mature "individuation"? No, he was actually revealing "infantile dependence," rather then the "mature dependency"
which would have been evinced, among other things, by promising a proper baptism. In the wisdom of mid-century psychology, "the rebellious person is also an immature person," just as
certainly as was the sissified bachelor who could not part from
his mother.

The difficulty in dealing with male rebelliousness, either on
the scale of the individual, or as some psychiatrists feared, of

the epidemic, was that it did have a certain seductive appeal. Women, too, were supposed to renounce many pleasures on the route to mature femininity—such as clitoral sexuality and petty career ambitions. No psychiatrist doubted, though, that the satisfactions of childbearing and mature vaginal sexuality would make up for these developmental sacrifices. Any lingering inconsistencies could be accounted for by the theory of female masochism, which conveniently transmuted the sufferings associated with the female sex role into pleasure. But men had no known capacity for masochism, just as they had no reliable instinctual drive to marry, hold down jobs and acquire life insurance policies. While a woman would be driven by her hormones to plead for a baby, a man, like the scientist in the case above, could imagine the alternative of a racing car. It was hard for even a mature psychoanalyst not to show a flash of empathy for his sex. "The male in our society is essentially a lonely being," Dr. Hendrik Ruitenbeek observed in 1963, "deprived of any real goal except that of acquiring the skills needed to make money enough to 'settle down' into an existence which he accepts rather than chooses."[17]

In an essay that must stand as a monument to psychoanalytic ambivalence, Kenneth Lynn began by indicting all the classics of American literature as tracts for male immaturity. Rip Van Winkle was not a harmless, befuddled old man; his twenty-year sleep was a deliberate escape from "the hateful responsibilities of work and marriage." Henry Thoreau was another "escapist," unable to adjust to the "quietly desperate world of work and marriage." "Almost every episode of *Walden* reveals," according to Lynn's reading, "an astonishing immaturity." This is the basic American character defect:

> . . . psychic immaturity. I say psychic immaturity because one of the signs of an undeveloped personality is the failure to recognize that serious personal and social problems cannot be solved by running away from them.

Only women writers had been exempt from this psychic immaturity, simply because it was so much harder for them to "throw over their responsibilities and walk out, slamming the door behind them." But when he came to explaining the childishness of America's male writers, Lynn suddenly softened. "The endless process of competing had become a waking nightmare," he said, "why should [men] continue to carry intolerable burdens, when they could just as easily walk out the door and start life all over somewhere else?"[18]

The ultimate reason why a man would not just "walk out the door" was the taint of homosexuality which was likely to follow him. Homosexuality, as the psychiatrists saw it, was the ultimate escapism. Asking himself what was the root problem afflicting male homosexuals, the distinguished psychoanalyst Dr. Abram Kardiner answered:

> They cannot compete. They always surrender in the face of impending combat. This has nothing to do with their actual ability, for many of them have extraordinary talent . . . These are men who are overwhelmed by the increasing demands to fufill the specifications of masculinity . . .[19]

These "specifications" had become so detailed and so rigid, that, according to Dr. Ruitenbeek, "it is not surprising to find an increasing number of men accepting homosexuality as a way out." Women were not tempted by a parallel perversion because they already had a relatively easy life: their "social-role expectations" were clearly "less demanding." (And, in case all this sounded suspiciously like an endorsement of male homosexuality, the psychiatrist hastened to add that the homosexual life was hardly a restful retreat, since it entails "compulsive sexual acting out.")

In psychiatric theory and in popular culture, the image of the irresponsible male blurred into the shadowy figure of the homosexual. Men who failed as breadwinners and husbands were "immature," while homosexuals were, in psychiatric judgment, "aspirants to perpetual adolescence." So great was the potential overlap between the sexually "normal," but not entirely successful man, and the blatant homosexual that psychoanalyst Lionel Ovesey had to create a new category—"pseudohomosexuality"—to absorb the intermediate cases. There was no "sexual component" to the pseudohomosexual's deviance, at least not if caught at an early stage. Rather, he suffered from some "adaptive failure" to meet the standards of masculine conformity, and had begun a subconscious slide toward a homosexual identity:

> . . . any adaptive failure—sexual, social, or vocational— may be perceived as a failure in the masculine role and, which is worse, may be symbolically extended through an equation that is calculated only to intensify the anxiety incident to the failure. This equation is the following: *I am a failure = I am castrated = I am not a man = I am a woman = I am a homosexual.*[20]

From here it was a short step to becoming an "overt homosexual," a man battered by so many adaptive failures that he "gives up all pretense of meeting the requirements of the masculine role."

If pseudohomosexuals could be treated by helping them overcome their adaptive failures, so could the overt homosexuals, since the two types were just at different points on the axis of masculine adaptation. Ovesey cites the case of an "overt" type whose homosexuality was just one part of a larger pattern of social deviance. The physical indications were promising; the patient was "23 years old, over six feet tall, good-looking, and completely masculine in his appearance." However,

> He lived alone and his social existence was a chaotic one, characterized by impulsive midnight swims and hitchhiking. He considered this made him quite unique and he was proud to be known as a bohemian.[21]

Furthermore, he showed no interest in a career, and supported himself as a stock clerk. The treatment (it is not told how he financed it) was both lengthy and stern. "The patient was treated twice a week, at first sitting up for 49 sessions, then on the couch for a total of 268 sessions over a 3½-year period . . . When, early in the therapy, he hopefully suggested that his homosexuality might be inherited and hence not amenable to treatment, he was told in a forthright manner that this was not so."[22] In Ovesey's hands, the patient made speedy progress. By the end of the first year he had given up hitchhiking and midnight swims, enrolled in evening college courses and gotten a more acceptable middle-class job. Eventually he married and fathered a son. With the developmental tasks accomplished, the case could be closed, and Ovesey must have been pleased that his equation checked out in reverse: I am not a failure = I am a man = I am heterosexual.

It is hard to see whom the equation hurt more—the actual homosexual or the "failed" heterosexual. In association with "failure," the homosexual's sexual practices became admissions of defeat; while in association with homosexual sex, failure was meant to be doubly humiliating. (Adaptive failure, Ovesey believed, led to dreams of anal rape by more powerful males.) Fear of homosexuality kept heterosexual men in line as husbands and breadwinners; and, at the same time, the association with failure and immaturity made it almost impossible for homosexual men to assert a positive image of themselves. Underlying both sets of sanctions was, of course, contempt for women; for in psycho-math, "I am not a man" = "I am a woman," which in turn, equaled failure, immaturity, mental illness and all the rest. To be hunted by bill collectors (one consequence of adaptive failure as a breadwinner) was like being penetrated by other men's penises: both were conditions in which a man became like a woman. Since a man couldn't actually become a woman (Christine Jorgenson was the only publicized exception throughout the fifties), heterosexual failures and overt homosexuals could only be understood as living in a state of constant deception. And this was perhaps the most despicable thing about them: They *looked like* men, but they weren't really men.

Near the end of *When She Was Good,* Roy Bassart finally abandons the dreary, uphill work of marriage and escapes to his parental home. Lucy now delivers her final denunciation of her feckless husband—not to him directly (he is afraid to come to the phone) but to his mother:

But he tricked *me*, Alice! Tricked me to think he was a man, when he's a mouse, a monster! A moron! He's a pansy, that's what your son is, the worst and weakest pansy there ever was![23]

In *Marjorie Morningstar*, the melodramatic best seller of the fifties, Herman Wouk passed a similar judgment on the errant male. Noel Airman is the great love of Marjorie's life and the object of her marital ambitions. He is everything that the earnest, stagestruck young woman might want, and everything her parents want her to avoid: glamorous, irreverent, vain ("Airman" is his fluffy, Anglicized version of Ehrman), irresponsible and bohemian. For five hundred pages she pursues him while he dashes between Greenwich Village, Mexico, Casablanca and Paris. She is dogged; he wavers between defiance and submission, even promising at one point to settle down to a corporate job. For a while their affair blossoms; then they break up with him marveling at "the narrowness of my escape." Reunited, Marjorie continues to press for a commitment; she is, after all, pushing twenty-four, and her thin talents have gotten her nowhere on Broadway. Again Noel escapes, leaving her with a punishing twenty-page denunciation of her bourgeois ambitions and the announcement that "I will not be driven on and on to that looming goal, a love nest in the suburbs. I WANT NO PART OF IT OR OF YOU, do you understand?" But what Noel doesn't understand is that time is running out for him, too; unfulfilled developmental tasks are piling up and the chance of achieving maturity is slipping away. When Marjorie tracks him down for the last time, in an apartment on the left bank of Paris, it is already too late for Noel; irresponsibility has taken its inevitable course to emasculation.

In the scene that is the denouement of their long and one-sided affair, Noel professes to be ready at last to settle down.

I'm ready to quit, Marjorie. That should be good news to you. All I want is to be a dull bourgeois. I've finally and irrevocably realized that nothing a man can do can make him stay twenty-two forever. But more important than that, and this is what's decisive, I've decided that twenty-two gets to be a disgustingly boring age after a while. Staying up all hours, sleeping around, guzzling champagne, being oh so crazy, oh so gay, is a damned damned damned damned BORE . . . I want to get some dull reliable job in some dull reliable advertising agency, and I want to drudge like a Boy Scout, nine to five, five days a week . . .[24]

This is the good news; the bad news is the new Noel. He chatters away just a little too gayly, flitting from restaurant prices, to the lotions he uses to restore his slightly receding hairline, to the source of Marjorie's new suit. He has become suspiciously domestic. In his Greenwich Village days, "he had been a competent slapdash cook . . . with a couple of specialties like spaghetti and southern fried chicken, dished up any old way. But all that was changed." Now he dons a well-worn apron and applies himself to preparing and serving a multi-course, haute cuisine meal. "Noel made a distinctly odd figure, scrambling into the kitchen, serving the food," Marjorie notes with discomfort. "He was quick and disconcertingly smooth at serving and removing the dishes."

The reason for his new attention to culinary detail soon emerges. He is being kept, in a sexually ambiguous relationship, by a square-jawed German woman with the ominous surname of Oberman. "What's the difference," he rationalizes to Marjorie, "whether the man owns the apartment and the woman cooks or the other way around?" If he doesn't know the answer to that one, in a novel published in 1955, he is clearly lost. Marjorie can forgive him for his domineering Aryan roommate, but not for his chicken in burgundy sauce. She rushes home, marries the first nice, stably employed Jewish man she meets and settles in New Rochelle to nurse her nostalgia. Noel, still broke and with no prospects, goes on cooking for Ms. Oberman. But even while thousands of co-eds were sighing over Noel's fate, other men were preparing to succeed where he had failed: to break with the responsibilities of breadwinning, without, somehow, losing their manhood.

EARLY REBELS
The Gray Flannel Dissidents

> The thing that makes an economic system like ours
> work is to maintain control over people and make
> them do jobs they hate. To do this, you fill their heads
> with biblical nonsense about fornication of every va-
> riety. Make sure they marry young, make sure they
> have a wife and children very early. Once a man has
> a wife and two young children, he will do what you
> tell him to. He will obey you. And that is the aim of
> the entire masculine role.
>
> —Gore Vidal, 1980

The gray flannel rebel lived by the rules. He accomplished his
major "developmental tasks" by his late twenties, found a wife
and made the appropriate adjustments to marriage, established
himself in a white-collar job that would lead, over the years, to
larger offices and longer vacations, bought a house, and nestled
into the "congenial social group" with whom he would share
highballs and the tribulations of lawn maintenance. He was
adjusted; he was mature; he was, by any reasonable standard, a
success as an adult male breadwinner. But (maybe because he
was just a little smarter than other men) he knew that something was wrong. It wasn't a material problem: This was a
time when the educated middle class worried about being *too*
affluent. It wasn't a political problem: "Ideology" had officially
ended, and the sixties hadn't begun. And it wasn't a psychological problem—unless the psychologists themselves were

woefully wrong about what it meant to be grown-up and male. The only word he had to describe the problem was one which, unfortunately, described everything and explained nothing. The word was "conformity," and in the fifties "conformity" became the code word for male discontent—the masculine equivalent of what Betty Friedan would soon describe as "the problem without a name."

But unlike women's unarticulated grievances, conformity quickly became a national concern. In June of 1957, conformity was the most popular topic for major speakers at college commencements. Robert Lindner lashed out at it in his popular 1955 book, *Must You Conform?*, denouncing the conformist male as "a psychopath"—"a mechanized, robotized caricature of humanity . . . a slave in mind and body . . . a lost creature without separate identity . . . a mindless integer . . ."[1] *Reader's Digest* covered conformity with a somewhat more temperate article on "The Danger of Being Too Well-Adjusted"; *Life* covered it; *Look* covered it. Brown tweed sociologists analyzed it, and their gray flannel cousins read about it on commuter trains or joked uneasily about it over their standardized screwdrivers and 4-to-one martinis. "The curious fact, perhaps," Daniel Bell wrote, "is that no one in the United States defends conformity. Everyone is against it . . ."[2] This unanimity was not so curious, if one observed, as many commentators did, that the ultimate "conformity" was the antithesis of Americanism and the trademark of Communism. *Look* magazine's 1958 feature on conformity, "The American Male: Why Is He Afraid to Be Different?" opened with an ominous invocation of existentialism and anticommunism:

> One dark morning this winter, Gary Gray awakened and realized he had forgotten how to say the word "I" . . . He had lost his individuality. In the free and democratic United States of America, he had been subtly rooked of a heritage that Communist countries deny by force.[3]

The answer, for the millions of Grays, was not to do anything nonconformist—like leaving wife and job to study Zen

Buddhism—but to at least be aware of the potential "I" sleeping within their pajamas. For most gray flannel malcontents, this was as far as their rebellion went: They cultivated an acute awareness of the problem of conformity—much as everyone else did—and achieved, through their awareness, a kind of higher, more reflective conformity.

Frank Wheeler, the hero of Richard Yates's novel *Revolutionary Road,* was a gray flannel rebel and a brilliant practitioner of this higher conformity. As a young man in the late forties he had once been a more authentic kind of rebel, living in a grubby apartment in Greenwich Village, studying at City College, and dreaming of the things he would like to write. An unplanned pregnancy had awakened him to the realities of male adulthood. Manfully forbidding his girl friend, April, to have an abortion, he married her and took a job with the Sales Promotion Department of Knox Business Machines, which he readily describes to his friends as "the dullest job you can possibly imagine." By 1955, Frank and April have two children and a spacious house located on "Revolutionary Road" above the mere developments and look-alike tract homes. He does not, however, lose sight of his youthful dreams; in fact, he incorporates them into his routine as an ironic counterpoint to the withering dullness and the "hopeless emptiness" of everything else. All day he works, or at least pretends to be busy at Knox Business Machines, and all evening he drinks with April and their friends, the Campbells, and regales them with his sarcastic commentary on middle-class conformity:

> Let's have a whole bunch of cute little winding roads and cute little houses painted white and pink and baby blue; let's all be good consumers and have a whole lot of Togetherness and bring our children up in a bath of sentimentality—Daddy's a great man because he makes a living, Mummy's a great woman because she's stuck by Daddy all these years . . .[4]

Frank takes the argument further, sounding a theme that will recur again and again in the fifties' literature of male protest. Conformity destroys not only men's souls, but their very manhood. Adjustment as preached by the psychologists was not the route to adult masculinity, but to emasculation. After a few more drinks than usual, he reveals this discovery to April:

> And I mean is it any wonder all the men end up emascu-
> lated? Because that *is* what happens; that *is* what's
> reflected in all this bleating about "adjustment" and "secu-
> rity" and "togetherness"—and I mean Christ, you see it
> everywhere: all this television crap where every joke is
> built on the premise that Daddy's an idiot and Mother's
> always on him . . .[5]

April takes this in admiringly. She wants him to get out before the castration is complete. They will go to Paris; she will earn a living and he will write.

But April is ahead of her time. Twenty years later, any sensible man would leap at an offer like this. It's what Frank *says* he wants to do, the only course of action his evening tirades on conformity lead up to. But Frank is terrified of giving up the security of Revolutionary Road and even more terrified that he has nothing to say in any forum larger than his own living room. Just hours before his epiphany on emasculation, he has decided to accept a promotion and stay on at Knox Business Machines. He will make more money, drink more highballs, and cultivate the ironic sensibility his dignity depends on: He knows he is being destroyed as a man, but at least he knows.

By the mid-fifties, dozens of academic writers had elaborated Frank Wheeler's alcoholic insights into a body of official wisdom. Sociologists in particular volunteered to serve as the critical conscience of the decade, periodically assessing the blandness of middle-class life and offering themselves as scientific experts on the penumbra of conformity that engulfed (other) white-collar males. Of these, none was more sweeping in his assessments or winning in his public delivery than David Riesman, whose 1950 treatise *The Lonely Crowd* was one of the rare works of sociological scholarship to become a best seller. Though Riesman's final judgment was ambiguous, his book reinforced the average gray flannel rebel's gnawing perception that conformity, notwithstanding the psychologists' prescriptions, meant a kind of emasculation.

Riesman's central thesis was that a new character type had appeared on the scene—the "other-directed" person. In the past, industrial society had spawned "inner-directed" people, who followed a course set early in life by stern parental authorities. Once his internal "psychic gyroscope" was set, the inner-directed man was relatively immune to the cavilings or nudgings of peers. He tamed frontiers, built up cartels or madly pursued white whales—whatever his inner script dictated. At best he was a man of great achievement and deep passion; at worst, he was a nut—obsessive, guilt-ridden, haunted by the inner voices. In contrast, the other-directed person, who was seen to be propagating swiftly at mid-century, was an easygoing, likable fellow. He took his cues from the people around him—friends, celebrities, the mass media— shifting his tastes and ambitions as the "others" shifted theirs. No deeper compulsion guided him than the need to "[pay] close attention to the signals from others."[6] By definition, then, the other-directed person was the familiar conformist.

Riesman was less than crystal clear in his analysis of how the American psyche had come to be, so to speak, turned inside out. Other-direction was, for reasons not fully explained, the price of affluence: "Hours are short. People may have material abundance and leisure besides. They pay for these changes however . . . by finding themselves in a centralized and bureaucratized society . . ." In this new society, "*other people* are the problem, not the material environment."[7] Fewer people work with *things*—machines, metal, earth—and more people work with, or on, other people. This analysis, of course, narrowed the field; welders, cleaning ladies and farm workers, for example, would have no reason to be other-directed. It was, apparently, only the middle-class, white-collar work world that called forth other-directedness in the souls of its inhabitants.

Within this world, Riesman's concern was further limited to the male sex (despite scrupulous referrals to the other-directed *person*). By way of explanation, he noted that "characterological change in the west seems to occur first in men."[8] In fact, a book on "other-directed women" would have been as unsurprising as a book on, say, fair-skinned Anglo-Saxons, because other-directedness was built into the female social role as wives and mothers. The traits that Riesman found in the other-directed personality—the perpetual alertness to signals from others, the concern with feelings and affect rather than objective tasks—were precisely those that the patriarch of mid-century sociology, Talcott Parsons, had just assigned to the female sex. In Parsons' scheme, the male (breadwinner) role was "instrumental"—rational and task-oriented—and the female role was "expressive"—emotional, attuned to the feelings of others. The other-directed *man* was a Parsonian *woman*.

In a Freudian scheme too, the other-directed man looked suspiciously effeminate. The inner-directed person was guided by a "psychic gyroscope" representing internalized parental authority and analogous to the Freudian superego. In Freudian psychology, which was known to the middle-class reader of the fifties at least in crude outline, only men had strong superegos, since only males had an unequivocal Oedipal crisis through which they confronted and internalized the father's authority. The other-directed man, like the Freudian woman, was pliable, uncommitted to internal standards of morality and achievement. Intuitively, or with the help of sophisticated interpreters like Parsons and Freud, Riesman's sweeping characterological transformation looked like nothing so much as the feminization of American men. (Interestingly, the one historical precedent for an other-directed society that Riesman offered was that of fifth-century Athens—a society that educated readers would associate with the acceptance of male homosexuality.)

Riesman himself never employed the obvious sexual metaphor for the inner-directed to other-directed transformation, perhaps because it would have been too patently judgmental. But his imagery hinted, not so subtly, that other-directedness was somehow less masculine than inner-directedness: The inner-directed were "hard" and confronted "hard" things; the other-directed were "soft," even "limp," and confronted only the "softness" of their fellows. "Today it is the 'softness' of men," he wrote, self-consciously enclosing the code word in quotes, "rather than the 'hardness' of material that calls on talent and opens new channels of social mobility."⁹ In a later interview he was more direct, warning that in our other-directed society, "boys can be boys only from six to ten" years of age. By implication, from then on it was not even certain that they would be in any traditional sense male.

Riesman was an ambivalent spokesman for middle-class male discontent. If, as a man, he did not like the "softness" of the abundant society, it was equally true that, as a liberal, he could not recommend a restoration of the "hardness" of the old days. Other writers, like William F. Whyte, author of *The Organization Man,* were angrier and more openly nostalgic for competitive capitalism and rugged individualism. The white-collar work world crushed initiative, rewarded conformity rather than creativity, and forced the individual to submit to the collective will of the committee, the "team." Perhaps worst of all, it was too comfortable, too easy. In *Life in the Crystal Palace,* Alan Harrington described his tenure at "a company whose products move easily in great packages across the continent" so that "there is no reason for anyone to kill himself through overwork"; mistakes will not be noticed anyway. In the sardonic spirit of Frank Wheeler, Harrington goes to work for the corporation just after selling his first novel, "a satire about a man, who, under the pressure of business, had turned himself into a Nothing." But it is not so easy to maintain his sense of ironic detachment; other-directedness sets in: "I became easygoing and promiscuously nice, and had a harmless word for everybody."

He begins to succumb to "the Utopian drift," the orgy of un-failing "niceness":

> If you have been in easy circumstances for a number of years, you feel that you are out of shape. Even in younger men the hard muscle of ambition tends to go slack, and you hesitate to take a chance in the jungle again . . .

After the image of impotence, Harrington escalates to castra-tion: "Apparently when you remove fear from a man's life you also remove his stinger." He can only assert his manhood through a tiny gesture: When the company offers free flu immunization shots, he refuses, choosing—absurdly—"to resist the flu in my own way," or—symbolically—to resist being pricked by the corporate needle, in final confirmation of his emasculation.[10]

Who was responsible for the sad state of middle-class manhood? If it was the bureaucratic work world that imposed conformity, then one might expect to find the culprits by searching higher and higher in the bureaucratic hierarchy. The radical sociologist C. Wright Mills had done so and discovered that there were real people at the top, a "power elite" that covertly ordered American politics, industry and consumer tastes. But his was a minority opinion. (Daniel Bell, the leading ideologue of post-ideological society, implied that Mills's intellectual perspective was similar to that of a derelict, someone who had tried to find "a place in society," but ended up in the apparently foolish position of "hating the bourgeois society" he is an unsuccessful member of.[11]) In *The Lonely Crowd,* Riesman scanned the upper reaches of power and reported back, with great certainty, that there was no one in the driver's seat, nor did there need to be: "While it may take leadership to start things running, or to stop them, very little leadership is needed once things are under way . . ." The fact that things get done, he continued, "is no proof that there is someone in charge." Surveying the society as a whole, he could find no human agents of power who could be either blamed or thanked by the "lonely crowd" beneath them. "Power in America," he said, metaphorically miniaturizing it to invisibility, is like "a molecule" and, as such, must forever elude the investigator's instruments.[12]

But the less sophisticated gray flannel rebel needed a scapegoat, and if the corporate captains were out of the bounds of legitimate criticism in Cold War America, there was always another more accessible and acceptable villain—woman. Hyperbolic estimations of women's power are probably as old as male supremacy; in twentieth-century America, the tightening grip of "matriarchy" was a favorite theme for male writers who aspired to be irreverent without being politically offensive. In the thirties, Stewart Holbrook had led the resistance, urging men to rise up against the indignities they suffered under a female dictatorship of taste:

> We eat lettuce sandwiches and marshmallow-whip goodies concocted out of the lethal columns of women's magazines. We play Ping-Pong; we knit and crochet . . . we even—God help us—launder diapers.[13]

In the forties, Philip Wylie led the charge against the megalomaniac Mom, who "is everywhere and everything and damned near everybody, and from her depends all the rest of the U.S." In the fifties, a whole posse-full of angry male writers took out after the American woman; if it wasn't the corporation that had emasculated American men, it must have been her.

The extreme position, taken by the incorrigible Wylie in a 1956 article entitled "The Abdicating Male . . . And How the Gray Flannel Mind Exploits Him Through His Women," was that women actually ran the corporations.[14] At the topmost reaches of power, where Riesman had seen only clouds of swarming molecules, stood the American wife triumphantly clutching her pocketbook. Wylie claimed that women controlled a full 80 percent of the money in America, enough to keep the nation's entire executive corps on its knees, pandering to her whims. *Look,* in its 1958 series on the American male, offered as evidence of the female takeover of the economy: "The number of women owning securities has increased 35.7 percent in the past four years, rising to 4,455,000. They own $100 billion worth of stocks alone." Women were credited with making 60 percent of all consumer purchases and participating in managing the funds in 71 percent of American households. Ominously (but, with hindsight, not too accurately), "the National Manpower Council predicts that an increasing proportion of women will hold authority-wielding executive jobs in the future."[15] For his part, Wylie felt that women did not have to actually take over corporate jobs to increase their power over the economy, they already had a winning strategy:

> The bulk of American women who do venture into the world-of-affairs do so to promulgate an *affaire* that will

lead to their early retirement as wives. Their mates soon die. The insurance is made out to the gals and the real estate is in their name. They own America by mere parasitism.[16]

A more moderate position was that women did not control the corporations, but they did control just about everything else. Thus, the corporate work world was actually a refuge—perhaps men's last indoor refuge—in a matriarchal society. As *Look* described man's flight from female tyranny:

> For a while, the male fled to the basement and busied himself sawing, painting and sandpapering. But the women followed him, and today they are hammering right along with him. No place to hide here.

Having exhausted the nooks and crannies in their homes,

> . . . some men are finding more and more escape in the pleasures and fraternity of corporate life. A large proportion of business is now conducted "in hiding" on the golf course and on all-male fishing trips . . .
>
> Men who can afford only a $1.50 lunch are spending three times that in fancy restaurants, and, when traveling, live in spacious suites, entertain lavishly and meet all kinds of interesting people. Home is never like this.

The corporation may have been the enemy of men's initiative, but it was men's ally in the struggle against woman, who was portrayed in cartoons as an oversized, dolphin-shaped figure, awaiting her late-arriving husband with arms akimbo. And if the corporate work world benumbed men's minds and crushed men's spirits, this too could be blamed on women. "Female dominance," *Look* opined, "may, in fact, be one of the several causes of the 'organization man' who is so deplored today. What he is doing is just building his own masculine world. His office is *his* castle . . ."[17] In a dizzying reversal of nineteenth-century domestic sentimentalism, home had become forbidding territory, and the corporation was man's "haven in a heartless world."

Another way that women were believed to cause male conformity was by driving men to meet escalating standards of family consumption. One of the articles in *Look*'s 1958 series on the American male credited wives with "the steady, if tacit, pressure . . . to keep up with those Joneses who always seem to be living next door."[18] There was at least a grain of truth in this. Even without the acquisitive Joneses next door, suburbanization guaranteed that middle-class men were not just working to keep food on the table, but to buy a second car, landscape the front lawn and stock the kitchen and basement with the kind of capital equipment that might (in an urban center) only be found in a laundromat or restaurant. For men, marriage and submission to the work world came together in the same package, so that if women were more insistent on marriage than men, they could be blamed for the entire male predicament.

In the fictional saga of a gray flannel rebel, *Revolutionary Road,* the wife does blame herself for her husband's discontent. It was her first pregnancy that precipitated their marriage and Frank's conscription into the white-collar work force. Now she begins to think that she should never have told Frank she was pregnant, and simply gone ahead with the abortion on her own. Looking back, she confesses to Frank that when she agreed to continue the pregnancy:

> It was like saying, All right, then, if you want this baby, it's going to be All Your Responsibility. You're going to have to turn yourself inside out to provide for us. You'll have to give up any idea of being anything in the world but a father. . . . That's how we both got committed to this enormous delusion—because that's what it is, an enormous obscene delusion—this idea that people have to "settle down" when they have families. It's the great sentimental lie of the suburbs, and I've been making you subscribe to it all this time. I've been making you *live* by it![19]

The only alternative she can think of—to flee both the house and the job to the acknowledged international capital of noncomformity—never strikes Frank as anything more than an unsettling fantasy.

The gray flannel rebel stayed where he was because he could

not think of anywhere to go. If he blamed the corporation for his emasculation, he was not about to leave his job—much less leap onto a soapbox and denounce corporate capitalism. If he blamed women, he was not about to walk away from the comforts of home (unless another woman, more compliant perhaps, was already in the offing). He was certainly not about to send his wife out to work so that he could take up abstract expressionist painting, or to suggest that women in general shoulder their share of the wage earning in the corporate work world. The gray flannel rebellion was never more than a lament, a critique far too diffuse to lead to action, stooping, at its lowest, to a nasty reprise against women, and rising, at its best, to sublimation in the "higher" conformity of self-conscious submission. Riesman's fainthearted alternative is representative of the impasse. Beyond "other-directedness" he foresaw the possibility of "autonomy." But autonomy, it turned out, meant only the inner freedom "to choose whether to conform or not." Nonconformity for its own sake would be perverse and "anomic"; the autonomous person, he wrote

> may or may not conform outwardly, but whatever his choice, he pays less of a price, and he has a choice: he can meet both the culture's definition of adequacy and those which (to a still culturally determined degree) slightly transcend the norm for the adjusted.[20]

Thus, the autonomous man turns out to be like everyone else except for some slight transcendence that distinguishes him from the merely adjusted—such as, we are left to imagine, an appreciation for Modigliani or an investment in psychoanalysis.

In fact, legions of intellectually minded gray flannel rebels saw themselves flatteringly portrayed in Riesman's "autonomous man" and settled down to cultivate their slightly transcendent tastes. So smug were they, so precociously mature, that no less a conservative than Norman Podhoretz was moved to excoriate their entire generation. "They discovered," he wrote, with characteristic sarcasm and an uncharacteristic note of radicalism:

that "conformity" did not necessarily mean dullness and unthinking conventionality, that, indeed, there was great beauty, profound significance, in a man's struggle to achieve freedom *through* submission to conditions . . .

A great many of them married early; most of them made firm and decisive commitments to careers of a fairly modest sort, such as teaching; they cultivated an interest in food, clothes, furniture, manners—these being elements of the "richness" of life that the generation of the 30's had deprived itself of.[21]

But Podhoretz could not think of any way out, either. The traditional mode of nonconformity, "represented by commitment to the ideal of the Revolution and an apartment in Greenwich Village," was as passé as hunger marches. All he could hope was that in some kind of miraculous rebaptism, the whole generation would decide to "break loose" in a vast primal surge and "take a swim in the Plaza fountain in the middle of the night."

But not every would-be male rebel had the intellectual reserves to gray gracefully with the passage of the decade. They drank beyond excess, titrating gin with coffee in their lunch hours, gin with Alka-Seltzer on the weekends. They had stealthy affairs with secretaries, and tried to feel up their neighbors' wives at parties. They escaped into Mickey Spillane mysteries, where naked blonds were routinely perforated in a hail of bullets, or into Westerns, where there were no women at all and no visible sources of white-collar employment. And some of them began to discover an alternative, or at least an entirely new style of male rebel who hinted, seductively, that there *was* an alternative. The new rebel was the playboy.

4

PLAYBOY JOINS THE
BATTLE OF THE SEXES

I don't want my editors marrying anyone and getting
a lot of foolish notions in their heads about "togetherness," home, family, and all that jazz.

—Hugh Hefner

The first issue of *Playboy* hit the stands in December 1953.
The first centerfold—the famous nude calendar shot of Marilyn Monroe—is already legendary. Less memorable, but no
less prophetic of things to come, was the first feature article in
the issue. It was a no-holds-barred attack on "the whole concept of alimony," and secondarily, on money-hungry women
in general, entitled "Miss Gold-Digger of 1953." From the beginning, *Playboy* loved women—large-breasted, long-legged
young women, anyway—and hated wives.

The "Miss Gold-Digger" article made its author a million-
aire—not because Hugh Hefner paid him so much but because
Hefner could not, at first, afford to pay him at all, at least not
in cash. The writer, Burt Zollo (he signed the article "Bob
Norman"; even Hefner didn't risk putting his own name in the
first issue), had to accept stock in the new magazine in lieu of a
fee. The first print run of 70,000 nearly sold out and the magazine passed the one-million mark in 1956, making Hefner and
his initial associates millionaires before the end of the decade.

But *Playboy* was more than a publishing phenomenon, it
was like the party organ of a diffuse and swelling movement.

Writer Myron Brenton called it the "Bible of the beleaguered male."[1] *Playboy* readers taped the centerfolds up in their basements, affixed the rabbit-head insignia to the rear windows of their cars, joined Playboy clubs if they could afford to and, even if they lived more like Babbits than Bunnies, imagined they were "playboys" at heart. The magazine encouraged the sense of membership in a fraternity of male rebels. After its first reader survey, *Playboy* reported on the marital status of its constituency in the following words: "Approximately half of PLAYBOY'S readers (46.8%) are free men and the other half are free in spirit only."[2]

In the ongoing battle of the sexes, the *Playboy* office in Chicago quickly became the male side's headquarters for wartime propaganda. Unlike the general-audience magazines that dominated fifties' newsstands—*Life, Time,* the *Saturday Evening Post, Look,* etc.—*Playboy* didn't worry about pleasing women readers. The first editorial, penned by Hefner himself, warned:

> We want to make clear from the very start, we aren't a "family magazine." If you're somebody's sister, wife or mother-in-law and picked us up by mistake, please pass us along to the man in your life and get back to your *Ladies' Home Companion.*

When a Memphis woman wrote in to the second issue protesting the "Miss Gold-Digger" article, she was quickly put in her place. The article, she wrote, was "the most biased piece of tripe I've ever read," and she went on to deliver the classic anti-male rejoinder:

> Most men are out for just one thing. If they can't get it any other way, sometimes they consent to marry the girl. Then they think they can brush her off in a few months and move on to new pickings. They *ought* to pay, and pay, and pay.

The editors' printed response was, "Ah, shaddup!"

Hefner laid out the new male strategic initiative in the first issue. Recall that in their losing battle against "female domination," men had been driven from their living rooms, dens and even their basement tool shops. Escape seemed to lie only in the great outdoors—the golf course, the fishing hole or the fantasy world of Westerns. Now Hefner announced his intention to reclaim *the indoors for men*. "Most of today's 'magazines for men' spend all their time out-of-doors—thrashing through thorny thickets or splashing about in fast flowing streams," he observed in the magazine's first editorial. "But we don't mind telling you in advance—we plan spending most of our time inside. WE like our apartment." For therein awaited a new kind of good life for men:

> We enjoy mixing up cocktails and an *hors d'oeuvre* or two, putting a little mood music on the phonograph and inviting in a female acquaintance for a quiet discussion on Picasso, Nietzsche, jazz, sex.

Women would be welcome after men had reconquered the indoors, but only as guests—maybe overnight guests—but not as wives.

In 1953, the notion that the good life consisted of an apartment with mood music rather than a ranch house with barbecue pit was almost subversive. Looking back, Hefner later characterized himself as a pioneer rebel against the gray miasma of conformity that gripped other men. At the time the magazine began, he wrote in 1963, Americans had become "increasingly concerned with security, the safe and the sure, the certain and the known . . . it was unwise to voice an unpopular opinion . . . for it could cost a man his job and his good name."[3] Hefner himself was not a political dissident in any conventional sense; the major intellectual influence in his early life was the Kinsey Report, and he risked his own good name only for the right to publish bare white bosoms. What upset him was the "conformity, togetherness, anonymity and slow death" men were supposed to endure when the good life, the life which he himself came to represent, was so close at hand.[4]

In fact, it was close at hand, and, at the macroeconomic level, nothing could have been more in conformity with the drift of American culture than to advocate a life of pleasurable consumption. The economy, as Riesman, Galbraith and their colleagues noted, had gotten over the hump of heavy capital accumulation to the happy plateau of the "consumer society." After the privations of the Depression and the war, Americans were supposed to enjoy themselves—held back from total abandon only by the need for Cold War vigilance. Motivational researcher Dr. Ernest Dichter told businessmen:

> We are now confronted with the problem of permitting the average American to feel moral . . . even when he is spending, even when he is not saving, even when he is taking two vacations a year and buying a second or third car. One of the basic problems of prosperity, then, is to demonstrate that the hedonistic approach to his life is a moral, not an immoral one.[5]

This was the new consumer ethic, the "fun morality" described by sociologist Martha Wolfenstein, and *Playboy* could not have been better designed to bring the good news to men.

If Hefner was a rebel, it was only because he took the new fun morality seriously. As a guide to life, the new imperative to enjoy was in contradiction with the prescribed discipline of "conformity" and *Playboy*'s daring lay in facing the contradiction head-on. Conformity, or "maturity," as it was more affirmatively labeled by the psychologists, required unstinting effort: developmental "tasks" had to be performed, marriages had to be "worked on," individual whims had to be subordinated to the emotional and financial needs of the family. This was true for both sexes, of course. No one pretended that the adult sex roles—wife/mother and male breadwinner—were "fun." They were presented in popular culture as achievements, proofs of the informed acquiescence praised as "maturity" or, more rarely, lamented as "slow death." Women would not get public license to have fun on a mass scale for more than a decade, when Helen Gurley Brown took over *Cosmopolitan* and began promoting a tamer, feminine version of sexual and material consumerism. But *Playboy* shed the burdensome aspects of the adult male role at a time when businessmen were still refining the "fun morality" for mass consumption, and the gray flannel rebels were still fumbling

for responsible alternatives like Riesman's "autonomy." Even
the magazine's name defied the convention of hard-won maturity—*Playboy*.

Playboy's attack on the conventional male role did not, however, extend to the requirement of earning a living. There were
two parts to adult masculinity: One was maintaining a monogamous marriage. The other was working at a socially acceptable job; and *Playboy* had nothing against work. The early issues barely recognized the white-collar blues so fashionable in
popular sociology. Instead, there were articles on accou-
trements for the rising executive, suggesting that work, too,
could be a site of pleasurable consumption. Writing in his
"*Playboy* Philosophy" series in 1963, Hefner even credited the
magazine with inspiring men to work harder than they might:
". . . *Playboy* exists, in part, as a motivation for men to ex-
pend greater effort in their work, develop their capabilities further and climb higher on the ladder of success." This kind of
motivation, he went on, "is obviously desirable in our competitive, free enterprise system," apparently unaware that the average reader was more likely to be a white-collar "organization
man" or blue-collar employee rather than a free entrepreneur
like himself. Men should throw themselves into their work with
"questing impatience and rebel derring-do." They should overcome their vague, ingrained populism and recognize wealth as
an achievement and a means to personal pleasure. Only in
one respect did Hefner's philosophy depart from the conventional, Dale Carnegie-style credos of male success: *Playboy*
believed that men should make money; it did not suggest that
they share it.

Playboy charged into the battle of the sexes with a dollar
sign on its banner. The issue was money: Men made it; women
wanted it. In *Playboy*'s favorite cartoon situation an elderly
roué was being taken for a ride by a buxom bubblebrain, and
the joke was on him. The message, squeezed between luscious
full-color photos and punctuated with female nipples, was simple: You can buy sex on a fee-for-service basis, so don't get
caught up in a long-term contract. Phil Silvers quipped in the
January 1957 issue:

A tip to my fellow men who might be on the brink of disaster: when the little doll says she'll live on your income, she means it all right. But just be sure to get another one for yourself.[6]

Burt Zollo warned in the June 1953 issue:

It is often suggested that woman is more romantic than man. If you'll excuse the ecclesiastical expression—*phooey!* . . . All woman wants is security. And she's perfectly willing to crush man's adventurous, freedom-loving spirit to get it.[7]

To stay free, a man had to stay single.

The competition, meanwhile, was still fighting a rearguard battle for patriarchal authority within marriage. In 1956, the editorial director of *True* attributed his magazine's success to the fact that it "stimulates the masculine ego at a time when man wants to fight back against women's efforts to usurp his traditional role as head of the family."[8] The playboy did not want his "traditional role" back; he just wanted out. Hefner's friend Burt Zollo wrote in one of the early issues:

Take a good look at the sorry, regimented husbands trudging down every woman-dominated street in this woman-dominated land. Check what they're doing when you're out on the town with a different dish every night . . . Don't bother asking their advice. Almost to a man, they'll tell you marriage is the greatest. *Naturally*. Do you expect them to admit they made the biggest mistake of their lives?[9]

This was strong stuff for the mid-fifties. The suburban migration was in full swing and *Look* had just coined the new noun "togetherness" to bless the isolated, exurban family. Yet here was *Playboy* exhorting its readers to resist marriage and "enjoy the pleasures the female has to offer without becoming emotionally involved"—or, of course, financially involved. Women wrote in with the predictable attacks on immaturity: "It is . . . the weak-minded little idiot boys, not yet grown up, who are afraid of getting 'hooked.'" But the men loved it. One alliterative genius wrote in to thank *Playboy* for exposing those "cunning cuties" with their "suave schemes" for landing a man. And, of course, it was *Playboy,* with its images of cozy concupiscence and extra-marital consumerism, that triumphed while *True* was still "thrashing through the thorny thickets" in the great, womanless outdoors.

One of the most eloquent manifestos of the early male rebellion was a *Playboy* article entitled, "Love, Death and the Hubby Image," published in 1963. It led off with a mock want ad:

> TIRED OF THE RAT RACE?
> FED UP WITH JOB ROUTINE?
> Well, then . . . how would you like to make $8,000, $20,000—*as much as $50,000 and More*—working at Home in Your Spare Time? No selling! No commuting! No time clocks to punch!
> BE YOUR OWN BOSS!!!
> Yes, an Assured Lifetime Income can be yours *now,* in an easy, low-pressure, part-time job that will permit you to spend most of each and every day as *you please!*—relaxing, watching TV, playing cards, socializing with friends! . . .

"Incredible though it may seem," the article began, "the above offer is completely legitimate. More than 40,000,000 Americans are already so employed . . ." They were, of course, wives.

According to the writer, William Iversen, husbands were self-sacrificing romantics, toiling ceaselessly to provide their families with "bread, bacon, clothes, furniture, cars, appliances, entertainment, vacations and country-club memberships." Nor was it enough to meet their daily needs; the heroic male must provide for them even after his own death by building up his savings and life insurance. "Day after day, and week after week the American hubby is thus invited to attend his own funeral." Iversen acknowledged that there were some mutterings of discontent from the distaff side, but he saw no chance of a feminist revival: The role of the housewife "has become much too cushy to be abandoned, even in the teeth of the most crushing boredom." Men, however, had had it

with the breadwinner role, and the final paragraph was a stirring incitement to revolt:

> The last straw has already been served, and a mere ten-
> dency to hemophilia cannot be counted upon to ensure
> that men will continue to bleed for the plight of the Amer-
> ican woman. Neither double eyelashes nor the blindness of
> night or day can obscure the glaring fact that Ameri-
> can marriage can no longer be accepted as an estate in
> which the sexes shall live half-slave and half-free.[10]

Playboy had much more to offer the "enslaved" sex than
rhetoric: It also proposed an alternative way of life that became ever more concrete and vivid as the years went on. At
first there were only the Playmates in the centerfold to suggest
what awaited the liberated male, but a wealth of other consumer items soon followed. Throughout the late fifties, the
magazine fattened on advertisements for imported liquor,
stereo sets, men's colognes, luxury cars and fine clothes. Manu-
facturers were beginning to address themselves to the adult
male as a consumer in his own right, and they were able to do
so, in part, because magazines like *Playboy* (a category which
came to include imitators like *Penthouse, Gent* and *Chic*) allowed them to effectively "target" the potential sybarites
among the great mass of men. New products for men, like
toiletries and sports clothes, appeared in the fifties, and familiar products, like liquor, were presented in *Playboy* as acces-
sories to private male pleasures. The new male-centered ensemble of commodities presented in *Playboy* meant that a
man could display his status or simply flaunt his earnings without possessing either a house or a wife—and this was, in its
own small way, a revolutionary possibility.

Domesticated men had their own commodity ensemble, centered on home appliances and hobby hardware, and for a long
time there had seemed to be no alternative. A man expressed
his status through the size of his car, the location of his house,
and the social and sartorial graces of his wife. The wife and
home might be a financial drag on a man, but it was the para-
phernalia of family life that established his position in the

occupational hierarchy. *Playboy*'s visionary contribution—visionary because it would still be years before a significant mass of men availed themselves of it—was to give the means of status to the single man: not the power lawn mower, but the hi-fi set in mahogany console; not the sedate, four-door Buick, but the racy little Triumph; not the well-groomed wife, but the classy companion who could be rented (for the price of drinks and dinner) one night at a time.

So through its articles, its graphics and its advertisements *Playboy* presented, by the beginning of the sixties, something approaching a coherent program for the male rebellion: a critique of marriage, a strategy for liberation (reclaiming the indoors as a realm for masculine pleasure) and a utopian vision (defined by its unique commodity ensemble). It may not have been a revolutionary program, but it was most certainly a disruptive one. If even a fraction of *Playboy* readers had acted on it in the late fifties, the "breakdown of the family" would have occurred a full fifteen years before it was eventually announced. Hundreds of thousands of women would have been left without breadwinners or stranded in court fighting for alimony settlements. Yet, for all its potential disruptiveness, *Playboy* was immune to the standard charges leveled against male deviants. You couldn't call it anti-capitalist or un-American, because it was all about making money and spending it. Hefner even told his readers in 1963 that the *Playboy* spirit of acquisitiveness could help "put the United States back in the position of unquestioned world leadership." You could call it "immature," but it already called itself that, because maturity was about mortgages and life insurance and *Playboy* was about fun. Finally, it was impervious to the ultimate sanction against male rebellion—the charge of homosexuality. The playboy didn't avoid marriage because he was a little bit "queer," but, on the contrary, because he was so ebulliently, even compulsively heterosexual.

Later in the sixties critics would come up with what seemed to be the ultimately sophisticated charge against *Playboy:* It wasn't really "sexy." There was nothing erotic, *Time* wrote, about the pink-cheeked young Playmates whose every pore and perspiration drop had been air-brushed out of existence. Hefner was "puritanical" after all, and the whole thing was no more mischievous than "a Midwestern Methodist's vision of sin."[11] But the critics misunderstood *Playboy*'s historical role. *Playboy* was not the voice of the sexual revolution, which began, at least overtly, in the sixties, but of the male rebellion, which had begun in the fifties. The real message was not eroticism, but escape—literal escape, from the bondage of bread-winning. For that, the breasts and bottoms were necessary not just to sell the magazine, but to protect it. When, in the first issue, Hefner talked about staying in his apartment, listening to music and discussing Picasso, there was the Marilyn Monroe centerfold to let you know there was nothing queer about these urbane and indoor pleasures. And when the articles railed against the responsibilities of marriage, there were the nude torsos to reassure you that the alternative was still within the bounds of heterosexuality. Sex—or Hefner's Pepsi-clean version of it—was there to legitimize what was truly subversive about *Playboy*. In every issue, every month, there was a Playmate to prove that a playboy didn't have to be a husband to be a man.

THE BEAT REBELLION
Beyond Work and Marriage

What is in it for the women who accompany the
Beats? The characteristic Beat culture, unlike the
American standard of living, is essentially for men
. . . Beats are not responsible husbands and fathers
of children.
> —Paul Goodman, in *Growing Up Absurd*

"Pretty girls make graves," was my saying . . .
> —Jack Kerouac, in *The Dharma Bums*

The gray flannel rebel resented his job. The playboy resisted
marriage. The short-lived apotheosis of the male rebellion, the
Beat, rejected both job and marriage. In the Beat, the two
strands of male protest—one directed against the white-collar
work world and the other against the suburbanized family life
that work was supposed to support—come together into the
first all-out critique of American consumer culture. Writing almost a decade before the emergence of a mass counterculture,
before Marcuse, before Woodstock, before hippies and flower
children, Kerouac had his Beat heroes refuse

the general demand that they consume production and
therefore have to work for the privilege of consuming, all
that crap they didn't really want anyway such as refrig-
erators, TV sets, cars, at least fancy new cars. Certain hair

oils and deodorants and general junk you finally always see
a week later in the garbage anyway, all of them imprisoned
in a system of work, produce, consume, work, produce,
consume . . .[1]

Life magazine woke briefly from the deep contentment of the
Eisenhower years, rubbed its eyes, and observed wonderingly
that the Beats were "against virtually every aspect of current
American society: Mom, Dad, Politics, Marriage, the Savings
Bank, Organized Religion . . . to say nothing of the Automatic
Dishwasher, the Cellophane-wrapped Soda Cracker, the Split-
Level House and the . . . H-bomb."[2]

If the Beats remained a minuscule minority, with scant appeal to most grown men, it was partly because of their rapid
media transformation into "beatniks." The original Beats were
men who criss-crossed the continent between New York, Mexico City and San Francisco, hopped freight trains, talked all
night over cheap wine, had visions, coined the word "beat"
(deriving it from "beatitude,") ate peyote and smoked pot,
had sex with countless women (and men), amplified all this in
a torrent of words (some written) and, when they were finally
singled out for attention, confused their television audiences
by talking familiarly about God and death. The "beatniks" on
the other hand ("beat" chastised by the addition of the Russian diminutive ending) were shortish sloppy men who appeared in comic strips and situation comedies wearing goatees
and sunglasses. The Beats were speedy, "mad to live," while
their images and imitators were studiedly "cool"—conformists,
like everyone else, but cut from a different mold.

The one thing they had in common, the image and the origi-
nals, was their rejection of the pact that the family wage system rested on. All of America could see that there were men
(and most Americans saw only the trivialized, beatnik version) who refused to undertake the support of women and
seemed to get away with it. In its semi-fictional 1959 account
of "The Only Rebellion Around," *Life* magazine claimed that
the really "successful" Beat got a woman to support *him*. *Life*
quoted "a North Beach [San Francisco] maxim," to the effect

that "the mature bohemian is one whose woman works *full time*." And lest this sound too appealing to work-weary husbands, it was noted that "the 'chicks' who are willing to support a whiskery male are often middle-aged and fat."

In their own lives, the leading ideologues and personalities of the Beat generation were indeed often irresponsible to women and vulnerable to every psychiatric suspicion about the "immature" male. Jack Kerouac had numerous liaisons with women while reserving his real allegiance for his mother, with whom he lived on and off all his life. Marriage and parenthood were beyond him. When his ex-wife tried to collect child support for their daughter, he first tried to deny paternity, then fled to avoid payment. William Burroughs killed his wife while trying, apparently, to shoot a gin glass off her head, and then promptly fell in love with a younger man. Allen Ginsberg flaunted the nastiest pyschiatric diagnosis; he was openly homosexual at a time when almost nobody found this condition "gay." Neal Cassady, the template for so many Kerouac characters and verbal inspiration for his best prose, loved women, even married two of them, but liked to keep a packed suitcase under the bed, ready to go.

It was not true, as commentators Gene Feldman and Max Gartenberg wrote in 1958, that the Beat male's rejection of marriage represented a nihilistic withdrawal from all human attachments, and that "he has no future which rests on a connection with some person or group . . . [so that] all men are the generic 'man,' all women the manipulatable 'chick.' "[8] The Beat pioneers were deeply, if intermittently, attached to each other. Women and their demands for responsibility were, at worst, irritating and more often just uninteresting compared to the ecstatic possibilities of male adventure.

In *On the Road,* Kerouac (Sal Paradise) and Cassady (Dean Moriarty) have a brief encounter with conventional morality as expounded by women. Sal has swept into San Francisco to pick up Dean, the idea being that the two of them should go to Italy together and generally do "everything we'd never done." Dean agrees to go, never mind that he is leaving his baby daughter and pregnant wife, who sobs relentlessly

while the men make plans. Later, on their way to one last
night on the town, the two men run into a group of indistinctly
characterized women, friends of Dean's wife, who lecture him:

> Dean, why do you act so foolish? . . . Camille called
> and said you'd left her. Don't you realize you have a
> daughter? . . . For years now you haven't had any sense of
> responsibility for anyone . . . You have absolutely no re-
> gard for anybody but yourself and your damned kicks. All
> you think about is what's hanging between your legs and
> how much money or fun you can get out of people and
> then you just throw them aside . . . It never occurs to you
> that life is serious and there are people trying to make some-
> thing decent out of it instead of just goofing all the time.[4]

Sal is irritated; after all, to him Dean *is* "the Holy Goof" and
these women are just "a sewing circle." Dean himself is un-
moved. He lets the women talk, and then walks out to wait for
the others to join him on the street:

> He was alone in the doorway, digging the street. Bitter-
> ness, recrimination, advice, morality, sadness—everything
> was behind him, and ahead of him was the ragged and ec-
> static joy of pure being.[5]

The Beat hero, the male rebel who actually walks away from
responsibility in any form, was not a product of middle-class
angst. The possibility of walking out, without money or guilt,
and without ambition other than to see and do everything, was
not even immanent in the middle-class culture of the early
fifties, when Kerouac wrote *On the Road* (which may be one
reason, in addition to the unconventional prose, why the book
was not deemed publishable for another six years, until 1957).
White-collar men fretted about conformity or fantasized about
"cheating" with the smooth, pink lovelies in *Playboy,* but there
was no real way out of the interlocking demands of job and
marriage. As Frank Wheeler had found, the road out of Greenwich Village went one way. The old-style Village bohemianism
—partly left-wing and partly pretentiously artistic—seemed
only quaint from the materialistic, anti-Communist fifties. The
new bohemianism of the Beats came from somewhere else en-

tirely, from an underworld and an underclass invisible from the corporate "crystal palace" or suburban dream houses.

Kerouac and his friends found inspiration in Times Square, not Washington Square, in Harlem rather than Paris. Dropping out from their own mostly lower-middle-class backgrounds, they worked, when they worked at all, as manual laborers, seamen or railway workers, and hung out in a demimonde inhabited by drifters, junkies, male prostitutes, thieves, would-be poets and actual musicians. They discovered jazz, and worshipped the great black saxophonist Charlie Parker. They were probably the first group of white Americans to believe that "black is beautiful," for blacks were, perforce, permanent outsiders, who countered their rejection from the white world by creating their own language and art. But if the early Beats went to the underclass, the underclass also came to them. In 1946, twenty-year-old Neal Cassady (Dean Moriarty in *On the Road*) arrived in New York, an ex-convict, inveterate womanizer and car thief, half genius and half con man. He looked like Paul Newman in *Cool Hand Luke,* and he talked with the easy, wild grace that Kerouac would adopt as a prose style. It was of Neal's meeting with Allen Ginsberg that Kerouac wrote the famous passage that came, for many readers, to define the Beat sensibility:

> . . . they danced down the streets like dingledodies, and I shambled after as I've been doing all my life after people who interest me, because the only people for me are the mad ones, the ones who are mad to live, mad to talk, mad to be saved, desirous of everything at the same time, the ones who never yawn or say a commonplace thing, but burn, burn, burn like fabulous yellow roman candles exploding . . .[6]

Others in the fifties were discovering the subversive masculinity of the blue-collar, or lumpen, male. White-collar men had all but admitted their own emasculation. And, for all of *Playboy*'s efforts, it would take James Bond and Jack Kennedy in the sixties to make Hefner's suave new upscale image of virility convincing to a mass audience. But in the fifties, the lower-class male who had never known the indignities of commuter trains and back-yard barbecues still seemed to be the last repository of defiant masculinity. Hollywood introduced a new breed of nihilistic, overtly sexual male rebels, who were either rejects from the middle class (James Dean in *Rebel Without a Cause*) or terrorists emerging from an invisible underclass (Marlon Brando in *The Wild One*). The scripts of these films were tracts for middle-class conformity: grow up, settle down and if necessary, betray the old, delinquent gang on your way upward to more acceptable circles. But the message was eclipsed by the macho beauty of the stars: Dean brooding and vulnerable; Brando with his head to one side, his eyebrow half raised in amazing arrogance.

Asked in *The Wild One* what he was rebelling against, Brando replied with an aplomb that would have delighted any North Beach Zen Buddhist: "What've ya got?" And of course there was Elvis, the truck driver from Mississippi who learned black music and shook up a generation of girls who had long since been reported lost in their reveries of wedding gowns and silver patterns. For despite all the developmental psychology and high school "life adjustment" texts, maturity just wasn't sexy, and adolescent defiance—symbolized by the tough, lower-class male—was.

John Clellon Holmes, a member of Kerouac's circle and author of the proto-Beat novel *Go,* grasped the affinity between the Beats and the fifties' undercurrent of youth rebellion. Writing in *Esquire* in early 1958, he acknowledged that most adults were "outraged" by the adulation of James Dean and Elvis Presley and "flabbergasted" by the rise of juvenile delinquency. He believed that the Beats were articulating the rebellious spirit represented by "rock and roll, dope addiction, juvenile delinquency, an amoral attitude toward sex . . ." and urged America's emotional grown-ups to take heed. Defending the Beats with an incongruously conventional morality, he asserted that they were neither "slum-bred petty criminals" nor "icon-smashing bohemians" but men on a quasi-religious quest for meaning whose findings might enlighten every middle-class person who agonized about conformity, that "growing collectivization of modern life."[7]

Most mainstream intellectuals were less sanguine about the Beats, revealing in their distaste a class enmity all the deeper for being inadmissible in normal terms of discourse. In mid-century America, the class that inspired the Beats was officially nonexistent. There was only the great middle class, and somewhere off to the side, the rich, still known benignly as "high society," as if wealth were an expression of membership rather than property. Nowhere in this flat demographic landscape was there room for Kerouac's "fellaheen" (literally, the peasantry, and for him, in a vague, non-Marxist sense, "the people," or the "real people"): low-paid manual workers, drifters, street people, migrant farm workers, loggers, prostitutes. Not until the sixties would middle-class America identify "the poor" as a category, and it would be still another decade before they concurred on the existence of a working class distinct from themselves. But in the fifties the notion of class was itself politically suspect, a leftover from the discredited vocabulary of left dissent. The "lower" class, denied a name or image, lived on in the middle-class male mind as a repressed self, primitive, dissatisfied and potentially disruptive. The Beats, whether celebrating the fellaheen, like Kerouac, or demanding an "affirmation of the barbarian" in all of us, as the briefly Beat Norman Mailer did, were an unwanted reminder of the invisible class outside and the repressed masculine self within. If they had been political in a conventional sense, offering themselves as champions of the proletariat, they would have been less, not more, subversive in an America that knew how to label, file and dismiss its "pinkos" and Communists. But the Beats spoke from an underclass of unassimilated people to an unassimilated corner of the middle-class psyche; and this, as much as the wanton beat of rock and roll, was dangerous.

Among the intellectuals, Norman Podhoretz led the attack. In 1957, recall, he had been chiding the young intellectuals of his class for their spiritual torpor, and prescribed a quick dip in a public fountain as a cure for the sclerosis of "maturity."

One year later he noticed the Beats and did a rapid about-face in an essay on "The Know-Nothing Bohemians," the Beat writers. Like John Clellon Holmes, he detected their covert connection to youthful unrest, but more in the spirit of a McCarthy aide disclosing a secret conspiracy: ". . . the spirit of hipsterism and the Beat Generation strikes me as the same spirit which animates the young savages in leather jackets who have been running amok in the last few years with their switchblades and zip guns."[8] Once the "young savages" have been introduced, the subject of the essay is briefly abandoned for a breathless, run-on excursion into youthful mayhem:

> . . . the gang that stoned a nine-year-old boy to death in Central Park in broad daylight a few months ago, or the one that set fire to an old man drowsing on a bench near the Brooklyn waterfront one summer's day, or the one that pounced on a crippled child and orgiastically stabbed him over and over and over again even after he was good and dead . . .

The language—"orgiastically," "over and over and over"— hints at some unthinkable vicarious approval. But the vantage point shifts back quickly from the young savages (and by implication the inner savage the Beats would invoke) to that of Podhoretz the intellectual and spokesman for his class. Now the Beats appear as Jacobins leading a mob of the unwashed against all that is decent and middle class, leading them, it almost seems, right to the door of Podhoretz's study, where they clamor brutishly as he writes:

> . . . there is a suppressed cry in [Kerouac's] books: Kill the intellectuals who can talk coherently, kill the people who can sit still for five minutes at a time, kill those incomprehensible characters who are capable of getting seriously involved with a woman, a job, a cause . . .

Never mind that Kerouac and his friends were themselves intellectuals and capable of talking (if not coherently by the standards of *Partisan Review*) for twelve hours at a stretch about Proust, Nietzsche, Rimbaud . . . or that Kerouac's work is singularly, even unrealistically, devoid of violence . . . or that a few years later, when Podhoretz was confronted with a generation that undeniably had "a cause," he would turn on them with equal savagery. He had established to his own satisfaction that the Beats were class enemies of the worst sort, foes of everything civilized, accomplices in every crime.

The lesser pundits of the mass media generally agreed with Podhoretz, and generated a series of feature articles that guaranteed the Beats would remain marginalized from both the gray flannel unrest and the inchoate youth rebellion of the fifties. The mass media's approach was subtler and more effective than Podhoretz's. He attacked the Beat writers head-on, with the blunt instrument of guilt by a kind of mental free-association. They bypassed the Beats to go after that more innocuous target, the beatnik. The Beats themselves were too elusive to make for crisp, straight-forward copy: What could you do with men who mocked the media with references to "fried shoes" or denunciations of "meatballism"? And they were perhaps too seductive in person. When pictures of Jack Kerouac appeared in newspapers after the publication of *On the Road,* dozens of women wrote to offer their bodies to this sexy new literary figure. The beatniks had no such allure. They were bohemians, of a sort, but without the passionate energy the Beats derived from a world outside the middle class. They were merely dropouts, declassé and slightly effete. By 1959 there were just enough real-life counterparts to the media's beatniks —college students and arty people drawn to the Beat centers of North Beach and Venice—to give the image credibility.

Playboy's assault on the Beats was complicated by an ill-concealed sense of rivalry. In his endlessly prolix series on "The Playboy Philosophy," Hefner grudgingly acknowledged the Beats as fellow rebels against conformity. He implied, however, that they were faint-hearted allies: " . . . modern-day nihilists for whom it was enough, apparently, to flout and deny." While the Beats dropped wearily from the line of march, the playboys had gone tearing on ahead. The difference, he argued, was that the playboys were ambitious; they wanted clothes, cars, fancy girls and they had the energy to get them. They were, in fact, Beats inverted—"Upbeats," as Hefner gleefully termed his own troops, who could work hard, seize responsibility and still "enjoy kicking up their heels."

It was in this last department, though, that the Beats might have appeared to have the upper hand in their imaginary factional dispute with the Upbeats. Real Beats kicked up their heels without any of the preliminaries of work and responsibility. In the area of sex, a case could be made that the Beats had a far better deal than the playboys. Neither believed in paying for it on the lifelong installment plan represented by marriage, but playboys still paid for it. (Consider the costs of warming up a date with an evening in one of *Playboy*'s own clubs: In addition to the annual membership charge, the amorous male would have to shell out a cover charge—plus an additional one for each part of the club he used during the evening—inflated prices for drinks and dinner, and tips for the bunnies.) Beats, as was well known, got their sex free, with no more financial foreplay than perhaps a bottle of California red wine, and even this could, with any luck, be left to the woman.

Thus, the burden of argument in *Playboy*'s February 1958 three-article special on "The Beat Mystique" was that although Beats had more sex than most playboys could ever hope to afford, they did not enjoy it. And they did not enjoy sex because they did not enjoy anything. To establish this, *Playboy*'s version of the beatnik had to be introduced, a man so cool he might have stumbled out of a cryogenics lab. One *Playboy* writer takes us to an improbable beatnik party, where, to his evident appreciation, "The swinging . . . really gets under way when one girl, or two . . . leisurely takes off her sweater or blouse. Then she takes off her bra, if she is wearing a bra . . ." The Playboy Club was never like this. But, we soon find out, such extravagant enticements are wasted on the beatnik partygoers: "The cats play everything cool—and especially sex . . . To reach out and grab a girl, a perfectly normal male reaction," the writer assures us, "is simply not with it, daddy-o." Another article in the *Playboy* trilogy on "The Beat Mystique"—this one by Herb Gold—suggests that the beatniks are more than cool, they are probably frigid:

> When the hipster makes it with a girl, he avoids admitting that he likes her. He keeps cool. He asks her to do the work, and his ambition is to think about nothing, zero, strictly from nadaville, while she plays bouncy-bouncy on him.

Playboy's readers could hardly envy the *Playboy* beatnik, a man who not only lacked "normal male reactions" when confronted with an unbound breast, but preferred the passive, i.e., female, role in intercourse.

Life magazine's 1959 attack on the Beats, "The Only Rebellion Around," by Paul O'Neil, was necessarily less focused on their supposed sexual deficiencies, but more wide-ranging and vicious. In keeping with the genre of late-fifties anti-Beat articles, we are first introduced to the beatnik, this time in a full-page graphic depicting "the well-equipped pad" and its occupants. Here there is no attempt to conceal the fiction; the photo, as the caption tells us, was staged with "paid models." To a viewer in the 1980s, it is a comfortable enough scene; in fact, the wood stove, the record albums, the espresso coffee pot and vase of what seem to be dried flowers, could be props in a trendy television commercial. But that, in a way, is the joke. *Life*'s beatnik, portrayed wearing "sandals, chinos and turtle-necked sweater and studying a record by the late saxophonist Charlie Parker," as the caption explains, is just a consumer like anyone else, a conformist defined by his own commodity ensemble: the "Italian wine bottle," "ill-tended plant," the "Beat chick dressed in black," guitar, etc. If this fellow is marching to a different drummer, we can be sure it is only because of his bongo drums, artfully placed in the center foreground. The one unsettling note is the "Beat baby" just to the right of the bongos, who, the caption tells us, "has gone to sleep on the floor after playing with beer cans." We are left unsure whether this beatnik is a harmless poseur or some kind of degenerate who can let a baby languish on the floor along with the "ill-tended plant."

Life staff-writer O'Neil was similarly ambivalent. On the one hand there were the dismissable, more or less harmless types, presumably the counterparts of the thin, self-indulgent young man in the photograph. These he described as the "sick little bums" who "emerge in every generation." Perennial malcontents, they might, in a more energetic decade, have been Communists or labor organizers, but for the time being, they were "talkers, loafers, passive little con men, lonely eccentrics, mom-haters, cop-haters, exhibitionists with abused smiles and second mortgages on a bongo drum." There is not much to fear from anyone who is "little" and "passive," or who, like *Playboy*'s beatnik, takes his sex lying down. The "Beat poets," actual, known men, present O'Neil with more obdurate material, and much of the article is devoted to defaming them with every psychiatric and juridical label available.

As a group they are "individualistic and antisocial to the point of neuroticism." Ginsberg spent eight months in a mental hospital. Cassady (misspelled as "Cassidy") was in San Quentin. San Francisco poet Mike McClure allowed himself to be supported by his wife, "a working school teacher." Gregory Corso had served time and never combed his hair. Ginsberg "repeatedly boasts that he is a homosexual." True, O'Neil reflected, some actual geniuses like Poe, Coleridge and Van Gogh have had their peccadillos. But even art cannot redeem the Beats, the bulk of whom are "undisciplined and slovenly amateurs." Overlooking Kerouac's wine and mother-loving tendencies, O'Neil attacked him for the amorality of *On the Road*. In the book, Kerouac had described a brief and loving stay with a young Chicana migrant farm worker. In *Life*, this episode becomes a soft-porn celebration of "the delights of drinking with cheap Mexican tarts." After surveying the Beat ranks of failed poets, psychotics, criminals and perverts, *Life* spoke for America: "A hundred million squares must ask themselves: 'What have we done to deserve this?'"

But no matter how busily the media diagnosed or dismissed the Beats, Americans could not simply turn their backs on them. Even that diminished Beat, the beatnik, seemed to inspire what *Life* called "a morbid curiosity." For the beatnik was not only a spectacle, half repellent and half exotic, he was also, even to his media creators, an imagined spectator—a vantage point from which everything normal became itself exotic or repellent. Within the beatnik—and essential to the beatnik as a stereotype—was the perception of the "square"—and it was the square, as much as his imagined antithesis, who fascinated. *Life*'s O'Neil was at his most eloquent not at describing the Beat(nik)s but at describing what he took to be their view of an "industrious square" like himself:

> . . . a tragic sap who spends all the juices and energies of life in stultifying submission to the "rat race" and does so, furthermore, with no more reward than sexual enslavement by a matriarchy of stern and grasping wives and the certainty of atomic death for his children.

Men looked to the Beats for a vision of themselves and, even after the imagined viewers had been discredited, the vision remained compelling. What the media said that the Beats thought about everyone else was, after all, not too far from what many men already suspected about themselves.

A *Life* magazine photo-essay entitled "Squaresville U.S.A. vs. Beatsville," also published in 1959, illustrates the power of the beatnik as imagined watcher. Three teenage girls in Kansas had written to Beat poet/entrepreneur Lawrence Lipton complaining that their town was "Squaresville itself" and inviting him to come and "cool us in." To the girls' surprise and their parents' horror, Lipton accepted—only to decline when the town fathers announced that if he showed up he would be summarily arrested as a vagrant. This brief contact between the Beat world and middle America inspired *Life* to give its readers a graphic contrast: Hutchinson, Kansas, versus Venice, California. The scenes from Venice include interiors from a Beat artist's "pad," a "ramshackle $75-a-month house, nearly walled in with huge abstract canvases," and a shot taken inside The Gas House (a Beat gathering place, sort of a noncommercial coffee house) and staged to arouse subliminal anxieties about dirt: A seedy-looking fellow is sitting in an old bathtub reading poetry while an artist squats nearby painting garbage cans. Arrayed on facing pages are the scenes from Hutchinson, Kansas, seemingly chosen for their bland wholesomeness: A family sits in a semi-circle, backs to the camera, watching TV; the town's bugle and drum corps marches down a main street; three paunchy retirees sit impassively on park benches. What is striking about the Kansas scenes is that they are so stolidly uninteresting—not news, not photographically ingenious, not even cute. Yet here they are taking up expensive space in one of America's largest circulation weekly magazines. Thanks to Venice, Hutchinson has become an event, a spectacle itself; and, seen from Venice, as the camera invites us to do, Hutchinson even achieves a kind of character in its dullness: This is "Squaresville."[9]

By the end of the fifties, the beatnik had even come to rival the psychiatrist as an imagined watcher—a critical vantage point from which it might be possible to judge what something *really* means." They each had their own arcane languages to describe, among other things, inner states that other people only felt. They each set themselves off as groups; the one, as a professional group with internal mores and hierarchy, the other as a subculture seemingly as exclusive as a profession. They had even come to resemble each other in affect: The stereotypical "coolness" of the beatnik matched the professional aloofness of the psychiatrist, serving in both cases as the mien of someone who can pass judgment without himself being judged, the face of "objectivity." And they each were highly visible cultural figures—for example, in cartoons and jokes— whom few people had actually encountered in person. Of course, these watchers were mutual enemies. What the psychiatrists found normal, the beatnik found square; and what the beatnik found hip, the psychiatrist would diagnose as illness.

A briefly famous psychiatric study of Beat society provides us with a vignette of the conflict between the psychiatrist and the Beat as rival spectators. In 1959, a psychiatrist, Francis J. Rigney, and a psychologist, L. Douglas Smith, brought the tools of their respective sciences to the Beat community of North Beach. Rigney spent several months observing the Beats (or beatnik imitators, for North Beach was already thoroughly commercialized) in order to categorize them and recruit subjects for individual study. Except for the slight loss of objectivity incurred by Rigney's necessary immersion into the Beat scene, everything was in order scientifically. Rigney developed a taxonomy of Beat types: "tormented rebels," "angry young women," "earnest artists," "passive prophets," etc.—and shunted representative individuals over to Smith to be given the Minnesota Multiphasic Personality Inventory, California Psychological Inventory, Thematic Apperception Test and the Rorschach test. The result, predictably, was that the Beats were crazy. As *Life* magazine reported it, 60 percent of the Beats were "so psychotic or so crippled by tensions, anxieties and neuroses as to be incapable of making their way in the ordinary competitive world of men," and another 20 percent were "hovering just within the boundaries of emotional stability."

But Rigney and Smith's voluminous data, published in their 1961 book *The Real Bohemia*,[10] make one wonder who exactly was being tested. Like the group of North Beach residents who, tired of tour-bus incursions into their neighborhood, rented their own bus and went on a flamboyant sightseeing tour of downtown San Francisco, the Beat subjects managed to transform their tests into a kind of spectacle. One complained about the quality of the artwork in the Thematic Apperception Test (TAT) (where the subject is asked to make up a story about a picture shown on a card). Another wrote in a TAT response that the characters depicted in the test card were too "middle class" and boring to write about. Another admitted his reaction to a Rorschach test was intended just to see the psychologist's reactions. Many used the TAT and Rorschachs to take off on long and seemingly unrelated poems or stories. A number expressed what Rigney and Smith took to be "cynicism," like the "earnest artist" who ended a TAT story with the question, "What does a test prove most, testee or testor?" Though Rigney and Smith ask us gallantly at the end to believe that the Beats are "above all, human beings," like good doctors advocating on behalf of the victims of some peculiar disorder, it is hard not to conclude that the testors have been taken for a ride. These "earnest scientists," as we might classify them, only establish that they are squares. And that, in large, was the Beats' lasting contribution to the male rebellion: to establish a vantage point from which the "normal" could be judged, assessed and labeled—square.

6

REASONS OF THE HEART
Cardiology Rewrites
the Masculine Script

> Medicine is a moral enterprise and therefore inevitably gives content to good and evil. In every society, medicine, like law and religion, defines what is normal, proper or desirable.
> —Ivan Illich, *Medical Nemesis*, 1976

The visible male rebels of the fifties were either disreputable, like Hefner, or marginal, like the Beats. In the family-oriented mass media, they could be dismissed, harangued or heckled with the full weight of psychiatric authority. Psychiatry represented medicine, which represented science, so that science was, at least by proxy, opposed to any deviation from the conventional masculine role. But science, even in the fifties, was changing its mind. Quite independently of each other, medicine and psychology (in America, the nonmedical version of psychiatry) were rethinking the masculine script and edging toward the conclusion that the rebels might, after all, be right. What had been defined as masculine maturity and understood as "success" began to look, in the light of new findings, like a hazard to men's health. And the early warnings came from the most respectable of sources, the medical profession.

Medicine was the last place that a male rebel might have looked for approval or support. If biology is destiny, medicine had never wavered on what the destinations were: for women, motherhood and homemaking; for men, fatherhood and bread-winning. In the crudest antifeminist biologisms, it is the unequal distribution of reproductive functions from which all else follows. Since women bear children they must stay at home with them; God gave women uteruses and men wallets. In the nineteenth century, medical science had established that it was not just the activities of childbearing and lactating that divided the sexes by function, but the potential for these activities. Women were innately frail, laboring as they did under a disproportionate burden of reproductive organs, and prone to innumerable vague nervous disorders and female complaints. The entire female life cycle could be described as a disease running its course. "Many a young life is battered and forever crippled on the breakers of puberty," wrote a president of the American Gynecology Society. "If it crosses these unharmed and is not dashed to pieces on the rock of child-birth, it may still ground on the ever-recurring shallows of menstruation.[1] The mere possession of uterus and ovaries con-demned women to a sheltered life, in which, if the financial sit-uation was propitious, periods of invalidism could alternate with mild diversions like shopping or visiting. It was fortunate that men were by nature "robust and striving," because women —even spinsters—required their life-long protection and sup-port.

Much of this ideology carried over into the twentieth cen-tury. Medicine continued to uphold masculinity as a standard of health, compared to which women could only be deviants, and to define pregnancy, childbirth and menopause as medical events, if not actual diseases, requiring sustained and expensive medical intervention. But the demographic facts gave less and less support to a theory of female frailty. In the nineteenth century, childbearing—especially when repeated at short inter-vals and compromised by poor nutrition—had put women at a biological disadvantage. Men outnumbered women and, on the average, outlived them. Then in the twentieth century, the pat-tern changed: heart disease, cancer and stroke replaced diseases like tuberculosis, pneumonia and other microbially caused illnesses as the principal causes of death; and in the face of the new killers, *men* were at a disadvantage. In 1920, men and women were running neck-and-neck: the life expectancy of women was 56, only two years longer than for men. By 1970, women's life expectancy was 75—eight years longer than men's.[2] Somewhere near the midpoint of this transition, the facts forced a major medical reevaluation of the relationship between gender and health. "You men," *Today's Health* told its readers in 1957, "are the weaker sex. Your average lifetime is about four years less than that of women. . . . You have a greater chance of dying in each of life's decades than have your womenfolk: Why?"[3]

One answer, popularized by Ashley Montagu in his 1952 book *The Natural Superiority of Women,* was that women owed their strength to their superior genetic endowment. Women have two X chromosomes; men an X and a Y, and the Y chromosome is only a deficient version of an X, "a wretched-looking runt compared with the well-upholstered other chromosomes!" in Montagu's judgment, "really a sad affair." A feminist in his leanings, Montagu specifically refuted what he saw as the common belief that men died younger because they worked harder than women. Male fetuses and male newborns are more likely to die than their female counterparts, and, he observed, they are not known to work harder. It was to their genetic deficiency "that almost all the troubles to which the male falls heir may be traced, and to the presence of two well-appointed, well-furnished X chromosomes that the female owes her biological superiority."[4]

In the 1950s, medical opinion began to shift from genetic to psychosocial explanations of men's biological frailty: There was something wrong with the way men lived, and the diagnosis of what was wrong came increasingly to resemble the popular (at least among men) belief that men "died in the harness," destroyed by the burden of responsibility. The disease which most clearly indicted the breadwinning role, and which became emblematic of men's vulnerability in the face of bureaucratic capitalist society, was coronary heart disease.

Death rates from coronary heart disease had risen precipitously from the 1920s to the 1950s, and it was in the fifties and early sixties that physicians began to speak of an "epidemic," and identify heart disease as "the number one public health problem," and even, in the words of two South African cardiologists, "the scourge of Western civilization." It was, statistically, a male disease; men were three times more likely than women to succumb "prematurely," or in middle age. And it was, in medical opinion as well as popular mythology, a middle- to upper-class disease, despite the lack of evidence that the disease was distributed in anything but the most democratic fashion, at least among American men.[5] Physicians spoke of it as a "disease of affluence" or the "executive disease," and articles directed at the public invariably portrayed the man at risk as a successful upper-level white-collar worker and a responsible family man.

The imaginary localization of coronary heart disease in the more fortunate members of society was, in part, self-serving propaganda for the class that included physicians as well as executives. "Much as an employee may have his doubts about it," advised one popular book on heart disease, "leadership has its price."[6] But, as the "price of success," coronary heart disease represented a gloomy new assessment of the meaning of success in what was, at least on the surface, an abundant and expansive society. The victim might appear to be in the prime of health, like, for example, thirty-eight-year-old heart attack victim "Paul Becker," profiled in *McCall's* in 1964, who was "a charmer, effervescent, warm, restless. . . ." Whatever he touched "turned to gold":

> His children were born in perfect pattern: boy, girl, boy. He started his own business, and it prospered. He was ambitious, and so was his wife, Janet. First came the dark little city apartment, then the shabby rented house in the suburbs, finally the low-lying modern home at the edge of the water. There had been a canoe, an outboard motor, and now a small yacht. Becker exulted that he would make his first million before he was 40.[7]

But, as a 1964 book by a businessman-turned-amateur cardiologist warned, "Coronary disease is a *hidden* disease, increasing the blockage year by year, *secretly*."[8] What Becker did not realize was that unseen fatty substances were building up in his blood almost in proportion to his external success. Blood fat, along with its companion cholesterol, was a kind of *inner* affluence, and like the external wealth described by John Kenneth Galbraith in *The Affluent Society,* it was wealth turned to waste, affluence turned to *refuse.** It built up, like the pollution in America's streams and rivers, until it choked the arteries which feed the living tissue of the heart. In a heart attack, part of the heart would actually die from lack of blood supply. It was as if, in a society and a class where there seemed to be a surfeit of things to eat and objects to consume, the hearts of men were starving.

* * *

In May 1955 *Life* magazine presented the story of "A Stricken Man and His Heart," which illustrated the terrifying new vulnerability of the middle-class male and pointed, indirectly, to the causes. Subtitled "A Commuter Has an Experience That Thousands Face Annually," the story begins with the forty-one-year-old hero, in evidently perfect health, speeding home from work on a late train to Connecticut.[10] The pain "arrived full-grown. It was as though a small hot bulb had suddenly started to glow in his chest. . . . Then he noticed that his left arm was numb. . . . He knew then, beyond doubt, what was happening to him." He asks an elderly woman sitting next to him for help, but, with the assurance born of cardiological superiority, she commands him "in a strong British accent" to "lean back and rest. . . . You are going to be quite

* Here is Galbraith's description of the "average" family on an outing in the fifties:

"The family takes its mauve and cerise, air-conditioned, power-steered and power-braked automobile out for a tour [and] passes through cities that are badly paved, made hideous by litter, blighted buildings, billboards . . . They pass on into a countryside that has been rendered largely invisible by commercial art . . . They picnic on exquisitely packaged food from a portable icebox by a polluted stream and go on to spend the night at a park which is a menace to public health and morals. Just before dozing off on an air mattress, beneath a nylon tent, amid the stench of decaying refuse, they may reflect vaguely on the curious unevenness of their blessings."[9]

all right." Though he can barely walk, he gets off the train at a station in the Bronx. Now he finds that illness has stripped away the prerogatives of class. A policeman mistakes his incapacity for drunkenness and only after an agonizing delay drives him to a public hospital, where he is thrown into an open ward with fifty other men. His condition is repeatedly contrasted to the strength of women. A woman doctor examines him "with narrowed eyes"; two female hospital attendants put him on a stretcher and "pull his clothing off him"; when he is released after forty-six days, his wife drives home with him stretched out in the back of the station wagon. What had happened was a "classic heart attack," of the kind which strikes "hundreds of thousands" annually, reducing them, in the space of a few minutes, from productive manhood to a state of dependency once reserved for women and children.

"The root cause," *Life* told its readers, was cholesterol. But the commuter's story offered other clues. He was a moderate man, who occasionally played golf, liked to fish and restricted himself to one cocktail and one pack of filter-tip cigarettes a day—austere rations by the urban standards of the fifties. He was not overly driven by ambition, in fact, he liked to "putter[ed] gently around the house and garden on weekends." Yet, there was a blot on his otherwise uneventful medical history: he had a "nervous stomach" and sometimes the pressures of work followed him all the way to his exurban home. When we meet him (he is unnamed in this otherwise "factually true narrative"), he is leaving work at 7:55 P.M. after working three eleven-hour days in a row. There must have been, somewhere in this man's activities and habits, a causative agent every bit as lethal as cholesterol, but it went unnamed until in 1956 Dr. Hans Selye publicized the malignant effects of *stress*.

Stress and the White-collar Male

It was not enough to blame heart disease on overwork because the group that was considered most vulnerable was also the group that did the least visible, least tangible work that an adult could perform. Both male blue-collar workers and housewives performed manual labor that had visible—at least briefly visible—impact on the material world and palpable impact on their bodies. They experienced physical tiredness, and this could be measured, if necessary, as the build-up of lactic acid in their muscles. But the efforts of white-collar males, especially in managerial jobs, were largely invisible; some malcontents like Alan Harrington or the fictional Frank Wheeler expressed doubts as to whether they were doing anything at all. Their labor had a ghostly quality that made it hard to quantify and even harder to link to the biochemistry of blood and tissues. The beauty of stress in explaining the cardiological fragility of white-collar males was, first, that it provided a bridge between vague emotional states and observable physiological change and, second, that it killed without any effort on the part of its victims.

Very simply, Dr. Selye's contribution to cardiology was the observation that if small mammals are sufficiently and scientifically abused, they will drop dead of heart failure, very much like harried human males. In the laboratory, rats and other animals were first disconcerted with injections of hormones and salts, and then subjected to various torments:

> Some were taped firmly to boards. Some were made to swim for several minutes in cold water. Others were placed in refrigerators and then quickly warmed up in hot chambers. Some were made to run for hours at a time in motor-driven cages.[11]

Dr. Selye labeled the cause of death "stress," and the actual torments "stressors" Extrapolating to the ordinarily less violent situation of human beings, he proposed that all kinds of annoyances may act as stressors (his students, *Newsweek* reported, called him "Dr. Stressor") causing hidden, incremental damage to the internal organs. Stress was the mysterious factor that, in combination with fatty derangements of the blood chemistry, sent strong men to their graves.

As a scientific concept—or as a practical guide to preventive health—stress left much to be desired. Physiologists had known since the nineteenth century that sudden emotions (fear, rage, sexual excitement) produce a predictable pattern of physiological responses—rapid heartbeat, raised adrenaline, etc. Selye's contribution was to add that prolonged or repeated emotional excitement, such as the terror and frustration experienced by his laboratory animals, produces observable, and sometimes fatal, organ damage. This in itself was an important observation, suggesting all kinds of mediations between environment, emotions and physical health. But "stress"—the mediating agent that Selye proposed—cannot be measured, detected or located in any particular set of circumstances, except in the most intuitive fashion. It was not easy to make the case that contemporary men suffered from any greater exposure to stress than their less coronary-prone ancestors, or that executives suffered more than janitors. Fred Kerner, who popularized Selye's work in a 1961 book entitled *Stress and Your Heart* (blessed with a preface by Selye himself) acknowledged the difficulty:

> Every generation has had tremendous stresses. There were stresses in the Napoleonic wars. It must have been very stressful trying to build a pyramid in the days of ancient Egypt. A Mayan Indian might have had his head cut off or been made a human sacrifice just because he happened to be on the wrong side of an argument, and this must have been a situation that was hyper-stressful.[12]

Selye compounded the confusion with his own ambivalence about stress. A vastly ambitious man himself, who at the peak of his career worked twelve hours a day and restricted himself to ten-minute lunches and "vacations" on a sun deck adjoining his office, Selye refused to condemn stress even after he had indicted it as a cause of disease. In fact, he delighted in issuing such aphorisms as "the absence of stress is death" and "stress is the spice of life." To clear things up, he eventually distinguished between "eustress," which is pleasant and healthful, like the excitement of winning a scientific prize, and "distress," which is what its name implies. The only way to distinguish them was that the good stresses ("stress of joy," "stress of victory," "stress of creativity," etc.) felt better than the distresses ("stress of deprivation," "stress of monotony," etc.).

Yet stress entered the culture in the fifties as if it were a powerful new paradigm for understanding the human condition. What it did explain, or at least justify, was the condition of the swelling number of white-collar corporate managerial employees. If they produced nothing—or nothing visible—and if they never exerted themselves in the tradition of "honest labor," still they experienced stress, and stress, like heavy manual labor, left its mark on the body. In fact, the concept of stress transformed the invisible mental work of the white-collar male into a kind of physical labor—a kind that was performed internally and without conscious effort. Selye called it "the wear and tear of life," suggesting the winding-down of invisible machinery within the body. Fred Kerner explained that "a ditchdigger rarely has a coronary because physical work is readily compensated for by food and sleep." Not so, however, with the abstract labors of "men under occupational stress who are straining to keep up with the Joneses . . . and to get ahead." Neither food nor sleep could compensate for their efforts, making them "the more likely sufferers of coronary heart attack." The ditchdigger might refresh his tired muscles with rest and a meal, but the heart of the mental worker—with its stress-choked arteries—was always hungry.

The wife of the white-collar male, the beneficiary of his stressful labor and of course his life-insurance policy, was as exempt from cardiological damage as the ditchdigger. Kerner explained the unequal distribution of stress between the sexes in terms of their economic relationship: Not only were men subjected to a more stressful occupation than homemaking, but they had the added stress of responsibility for the home*maker:*

> It seems that being the breadwinner—whether man or woman—is a difficult job. Tension is inevitable. The job of homemaker, on the other hand, gives the woman some time—if she desires it—to relax and let some things go. She can often find time for interesting hobbies right at home. She can vary her activities. She can usually take time to rest during the day. This is not so with the bread-

winner. The family's livelihood and security hinge on the way the breadwinner handles his job. . . . Just the realization of the responsibility is enough to make many men feel tense and anxious at all times.[18]

In *McCall's* 1964 scare story on "Five Husbands Who Might Have Lived," all five were outstanding breadwinners, stuck, in four of the cases, with wives who were either pushy or "infantile." "Joseph Fowler," thirty-eight, was the vice-president of a brokerage firm and a doting husband: "He worshiped Muriel. . . . Alone, he managed their financial affairs, paid the bills, gave her a weekly allowance, just as he gave his sons spending money." In a friend's post-mortem observation, "He wanted to protect her." But, as Fowler's physician knew, his "coronary arteries . . . were narrow, roughened, with fatty deposits clinging to their walls" and there was no one to protect him when the arteries suddenly clamped shut, strangling his heart.

Or take "Thomas Langdon," forty-four:

> He worked hard, stopping only for a sandwich at his desk when he was not lunching with clients. You have to work hard to live as the Langdons did. Mrs. Langdon dressed exquisitely. Their two sons attended expensive prep schools.

Langdon suffered from angina, a warning that the arteries which "feed the heart bright red oxygenated blood are too narrow to cope," but he was unable to follow the low-fat diet prescribed for him. "How can I eat grass for dinner when she has a steak with bearnaise sauce?" he complained to his doctor. Then, one night after dinner:

> Mrs. Langdon showed her husband the leopard coat she had just purchased. He upbraided her for being extravagant. They both yelled. In the middle of a cutting remark, he sat down hard in a chair. He never got up.

There is no doubt that the lives of ambitious white-collar men are, in some intuitive sense, stressful, but given the murkiness of the concept of stress, there was no way to know whether these men actually experienced more stress than their wives (especially since Selye had acknowledged "boredom" as a stressor) or whether it was the stress, rather than, say, the bearnaise sauce, that killed them. Yet the idea that there is a special, lethal kind of stress associated with the breadwinner's role is so firmly fixed in medical opinion that it has withstood both the absence of supporting evidence and the presence of contradictory evidence. In the mid-1970s, when women's work force participation rose to 50 percent, the medical profession issued stern warnings that women were either about to or were already experiencing their own epidemic of coronary heart disease. A "heart expert," Dr. Eugene Schiemann, was quoted in the New York *Daily News* as saying that, "As more women abandon their protected roles and enter the competitive mainstream, [their] rate of coronaries is increasing." The respected epidemiologist Leo Reeder told a 1976 meeting of the American Sociological Association that women's death rate from coronary heart disease was rising in response to their changing life-styles. Women's magazines featured dozens of articles on the new threat of stress—the "price of success" and the source of "lib sickness." Even the now venerable Dr. Selye warned, "The more the 'Women's Liberation' movement permits women to take what have usually been considered male jobs, the more women are subject to so-called male diseases, such as cardiac infarctions, gastric ulcers, and hypertension. They get the same satisfactions, too, of course, but at a price."[14]

In fact, women suffered no increase in coronary heart disease—or any other disease thought to be stress-related—as a result of their influx into the work force in the sixties and seventies. If anything, women's health improved relative to men's: In 1960, males were 1.62 times as likely as females to die of coronary heart disease; in 1976, males were 2.1 times as likely to die of heart disease. (The only disease category in which women lost ground was lung cancer, and that was because women of all ages, employed and unemployed, were smoking more.) A mammoth eight-year study of 900 women in Framingham, Massachusetts, released by the National Heart, Lung and Blood Institute in 1979, showed that women employed outside the home were no more likely to develop coronary heart disease than full-time housewives.[15] Where had the doctors gotten the idea of a female coronary epidemic? Well, confronted by an inquiring young sociologist, Dr. Reeder confessed that he could not recall the source of his information on women's rising mortality from coronary heart disease.[16] The "heart expert" Dr. Eugene Scheimann, whom I traced to Chicago, turned out to be an eighty-two-year-old general practitioner and a member of the advisory board of *Penthouse*'s *Forum* magazine. His only claim to cardiological expertise was his authorship of a book entitled *Sex Can Save Your Heart*. When asked for his references, he told me, "I don't believe in statistics. Women have more love problems than men, and now they have the stresses of work too. That is why they are dying." Such are the folkloric sources of medical opinion.

In the 1950s and 1960s, before women's employment became a matter for medical concern, physicians were inevitably drawn to the question of why some men succumbed and others, presumably exposed to equal doses of stress, survived. The coronary victims profiled in popular magazines were invariably hardworking, successful family men—models, in fact, of mature masculinity. It was hard to avoid the suspicion that —along with fatty foods, tobacco and a stress-filled white-collar occupation—masculinity itself might be a risk factor for coronary heart disease. To famed cardiologist Paul Dudley White, coronary patients looked more "robust" and "masculine" than other men. In a *Ladies' Home Journal* article entitled "Be Glad You're a Woman—You'll Live Longer," cardiologist Howard Sprague revealed that in his experience, the "most physically 'masculine' males were most susceptible."[17] Furthermore, some doctors cited the case of "a eunuch colony in Kansas" whose inmates were apparently free of the disease and revealed, upon autopsy, healthy, unencumbered coronary arteries. If eunuchs and women were relatively immune, it seemed to follow that among anatomically intact men, the "best" and most manly were the most vulnerable.

This inference shaped the remarkable work of Dr. Daniel Schneider. A psychoanalyst, he approached the coronary epidemic with a certain entrepreneurial interest: Cardiologists, he believed, were missing the boat because they had neglected the contributions of psychoanalysis (to give the psyche its due, he suggested that heart attacks should be renamed "brain-heart attacks"). Psychoanalysts, on the other hand, had neglected the heart for other organs unduly favored by Freud; in Schneider's scheme the heart loomed (or, to use his imagery, boomed) larger in men's psyches than the phallus. To bridge the gap between the disciplines, he put forth as a "principle" the tautological proposition that "the heart-brain, brain-mind, and mind-heart are indispensable parts of one single mechanism because the brain is primarily a cardiopsychic instrument."[18]

This merger of heart and brain threw a new light on male deviants: They were avoiding not just responsibility, but heart disease. The homosexual was a man who "little by little . . . slips away from the reality of his shape and genital equipment" in order to "separate[s] his heart from the danger of masculinity." This was a symbolic evasion, as well as a preventive-health measure, for the heartbeat signifies time/mortality/death/birth and hence, according to psychoanalytic logic, heterosexuality. In one case studied by Dr. Schneider, a bout of rheumatic fever had been sufficient to scare a man out of heterosexuality. It followed that the ultimate preventive measure would be to actually remove the penis to save the heart. "A puzzling phenomenon of modern psychiatry is that certain utterly robust and masculine men present themselves for operation . . . *to be converted into women.*" Not so puzzling, though, if you considered the probable health benefits of this cowardly operation. Transsexuals, Schneider opined,

> . . . apparently will not die of coronary disease. . . . They have cured the problem of their cholesterol, their uric acid, their sugar, their phospholipides. . . . The heart goes scot-free in girlish ways. The stress endured by the robust and masculine is over.[19]

For better or worse, Schneider's cardiopsychic theory had little impact on his fellow physicians, but it did illustrate the gloomy impasse cardiology came to when it pondered the psychosocial sources of heart disease. The most hazardous environment turned out to be the one that all men were expected to strive for—the home and office of the successful middle-class man. And the most vulnerable personality appeared to be the best adjusted, most responsible and clearly masculine. When it came down to a choice between the penis and the heart—and it took the psychoanalytic imagination to dramatize the choice—then the male condition was truly hopeless. Psychology was not ready to condemn masculinity as a health hazard, and medicine was not about to indict the corporate system for generating toxic levels of occupational stress. The way out of the impasse was to blame the victims, and to blame them—not for their masculinity—but for their "type" of masculinity.

The Type A Personality

With the discovery of the Type A personality, cardiologists had not found the elusive molecular "cause" of coronary heart disease—an excess or deficiency of some hormone, a defective enzyme or perhaps even a virus—but they could pinpoint the cardiac equivalent of "carriers," those superficially healthy people who harbor disease in a secret, latent form. The Type A personality, as cardiologists Meyer Friedman and Ray Rosenman defined it, was impatient, driven, hostile and competitive, as could be judged by simple observation or more objective psychological tests. Friedman and Rosenman had begun with the observation—perhaps familiar to physicians with a largely executive-class male clientele—that their own coronary patients tended to display all these unpleasant characteristics. For example, they systematically wore out the upholstery at the front edge of their seats, perhaps gripped with anxiety over missed deadlines and lost contracts. To test for a possible association between the Type A traits and coronary heart disease, the two doctors did a variety of studies comparing the cardiac status of Type A's with that of apparently more relaxed occupational types, such as embalmers and members of the Junior League. As expected, the ambitious and striving (Type A) tended to have more symptoms of impending or actual heart disease than the more phlegmatic or indolent (Type B).

The publication of Friedman and Rosenman's findings (within the medical profession in the late fifties and to the general public in 1963) seemed to advance cardiology beyond the vague notion of stress to something more modern, reductionist and clear-cut. Stress was an indefinable menace, like the miasmas and "bad airs" that scientists had held responsible for contagious diseases until the discovery of bacteria. Type A-ness, on the other hand, could be detected, just as bacteria could, at least so long as one was willing to credit psychological testing with a resolving power on a par with that of the microscope. (Even the nomenclature of two "types" was reminiscent of the familiar classification of bacteria into gram-negative and gram-positive types.) Yet it was never clear in Rosenman and Friedman's statements whether Type A was a congenital disposition or a behavior pattern elicited by certain stressful situations.† In a 1964 *Business Week* interview, Friedman and Rosenman stated that Type A was probably incurable, and that the most that could be done was to monitor the Type A man for any suspicious rise in blood fat or cholesterol.[20]

As a diagnostic category, Type A was unique, existing with-

† Nor was it clear what Type A-ness might mean for people other than middle-class professionals and executives. In Rosenman and Friedman's definition, competitive careerism was essential to Type A-ness, and a more refined test later designed by C. D. Jenkins and S. J. Zyzanski emphasized intense "job involvement" as essential to the Type A coronary-prone personality. Yet people with unrewarding jobs that offer little opportunity for emotional involvement, as well as people with no jobs at all, also die of coronary heart disease. Epidemiologists are still divided amongst themselves on the relevance of the A/B typology to blue-collar males or women of any occupation. Yet despite all the scientific uncertainties, "Type A" quickly became a middle-class colloquialism and, for many practicing physicians, a kind of offhand diagnosis.

out reference to any known categories of psychological disorder. Friedman and Rosenman, perhaps fearful of intrusions by eager psychiatrists like Schneider, insisted that Type A was not a neurosis or a new name for a disease already claimed by psychiatry. In their early accounts, Type A seemed almost benign: Dr. Friedman cheerfully admitted to being an "A-man" himself and said he suspected the same of Rosenman, and together they estimated that as many as 60 percent of the population might be Type A. *Business Week* described the Type A man as a somewhat harried, but otherwise admirable character: "agressive, hard-driving, vigorously competitive, continuously subject to deadlines, and [subject to] an exaggerated sense of time urgency."

Clearly he was responsible and hardworking—in fact, he was *too* responsible and hardworking, and in a middle-class world that was still seeking a balance between adjustment and achievement, he was an *extreme*. C. D. Jenkins, who refined the Type A concept in the sixties, described the characteristics of the Type A personality as *"extremes* of competitiveness, striving for achievement, aggressiveness . . . haste . . . and feelings of being under the pressure of time and under the challenge of responsibility."[21] (Emphasis added.)

As a cultural judgment, what was wrong with the Type A man was not that he was too sensitive to the pressures of the white-collar work world, but that he was out of place in it. He was a throwback to competitive capitalism, a driven man, like Melville's Captain Ahab, but given, in the modern era, much smaller fish to fry. In a sense, the Type A/B formulation represented a medicalization of Riesman's inner-directed and other-directed categories, but offered, this time, with less ambivalence. The medical description of Type A suggested a misplaced obsessiveness—"restlessness, hyperalertness, explosiveness of speech, tenseness of facial musculature" in Jenkins' description—which had become mere habit, unrelated to external goals. Riesman's inner-directed man had the redeeming quality of depth—at least there was an *inside* from which he was directed. Cardiology, however, had the special advantage of being able to literally see the "inside," or at least to see the blood chemicals, arteries and the heart; and it had found these to be sick and failing. With the A/B typology, cardiology seemed to pass a final judgment on the inner-directed man; not only was he historically obsolete, he was marked for biological extinction. The better-adjusted Type B's might be duller and more shallow, like Riesman's other-directed man, but they had the cardiological advantage.

Relax and Survive

Friedman and Rosenman's work helped to marginalize the coronary-prone—even if it was to a potential majority of the population—and redeem the conventional notion of middle-class manhood. But in the popular literature on coronary heart disease, it made little difference whether the operative paradigm was Selye's stress or the cardiologists' Types A and B: The prescription for male survival was to relax and even to regress to a more feminine, dependent state. Men were urged to achieve eight or even nine hours of sleep a night and (this before doctors roused men from inactivity to run for their lives) to avoid immoderate exercise. Career aspirations would have to be lowered. "What's wrong with being second vice-president?" demanded Selye's popularizer, Fred Kerner. "You can't all be first!" Dr. Friedman confided in *Newsweek* that he kept his own Type A tendencies at bay by occasionally dodging out of a professional meeting to attend an art show.[22] The soothing powers of art were also endorsed by *Today's Health,* which urged men to cultivate such hitherto sissified interests even at the risk of male opprobrium. "If it is fun to daub paint on a canvas," a 1957 article advised, "go ahead and do it and let the other guys sneer!"[23]

While coronary-conscious males slumbered or dabbled in nonremunerative pastimes, the duties of their wives were expanding to professional proportions. *McCall's* told its readers that the answer to the question "Must men . . . destroy themselves?" lay ultimately with women: "Wives are the key." The medical profession began to recognize the wife as a new kind of ancillary worker to be enlisted in the struggle against the coronary epidemic. For every article on coronary prevention addressed to men, two or three appeared addressed to women, and in 1965, celebrity cardiologist Dr. Paul Dudley White made a special lecture tour for female audiences, attracting over 10,000 in Portland, Oregon, alone.[24]

First, according to the barrage of advice from the cardiologists, women had to master a new nutritional technology that had moved beyond the old "basic food groups" to fine distinctions between saturated, unsaturated and polyunsaturated fats. A husband's meals had to be engineered for survival rather than satiety, and sources of cholesterol, like the once-innocent egg, had to be gently eliminated. Equally important, household stress had to be monitored to prevent a toxic build-up in combination with the inevitable stress of work. "A wise wife," cardiologist Herman Sobol advised women in the *Reader's Digest* "will try to shield her husband from any *added* stress."[25] He cautioned against "the five- or six-o'clock frenzy" that greeted all too many men at the end of the day. Little children should be fed early and older ones dispersed so that Dad can "recover from the day" over his cocktail in a hushed and restful atmosphere.

The task of nursing a white-collar husband gave some much-needed new dignity to the housewife's job. If she was a parasite, as *Playboy* insisted, she could at least be a useful one, running her kitchen like a dietician and maintaining a hospital quiet zone around the tired breadwinner. With his fragility, her authority, too, increased. "A woman can be the dominating force in controlling the longevity of her husband," Dr. Edward Newman promised women in *McCall's*. The coronary-threatened husband would necessarily have to defer to the stronger partner, who was becoming, in a marriage now centered on cardiological prophylaxis, a "mother as well a lover." Of course, she would have to exercise her authority with discretion since, according to Newman, a man "must still be king of the hill." Similarly, *Reader's Digest*'s Dr. Sobol warned the cholesterol-conscious wife that "a male hates to feel pushed or browbeaten. When he's forced by his wife, the stress is likely to balance out any good done by the dieting." Wives could employ little tricks to head off stressful tantrums: "Rather than have scenes at the table about his eating the fat on the roast," Sobol advised, the wife should covertly "remove the fat in the kitchen."

But the diet and stress management and the sneaky subterfuges were all, in a way, temporary stratagems. The long-term effect of the coronary scare was to undermine women's claims to a share of the husband's wage and, beyond that, to indict the breadwinning role as a "lethal trap" for men. *McCall's* article on "Five Husbands Who Might Have Lived" could have been entitled "Five Wives Who Might Have Lived on Less," so zealous were the deceased in their breadwinning efforts, so complacent—or greedy—were the widows-to-be. In the early sixties, blame was still localized in the spendthrift type of wife whose craving for fur coats and bearnaise sauce drove husbands panting up the career ladder. When a female interviewer asked Dr. Sobol, somewhat plaintively, what else she could do in addition to monitoring her husband's physical health, he snapped, "Very simply, you can try to live within your husband's means." Within a decade even that modest project would be suspect, and the charge of homicide by heart disease could be leveled at *all* financially dependent wives. "Millions of women . . . still claim that they find total fulfillment as home-makers," writer Marya Mannes observed sarcastically in 1972, "even if the price of their fulfillment is the death by continuous strain of the men who provided it; even if the price be their own long widowhood."[26] Cardiology did not lead the attack on the homemaker as public health hazard, but it had, wittingly or unwittingly, delivered the supporting evidence.

The commuter hero of *Life*'s 1955 story of "A Stricken Man and His Heart" survived. When last we see him, convalescing at home, he has achieved a state of beatitude that Friedman and Rosenman might have rated Type B-plus. "Much of the time he sits reading in the sun, or only thinking. . . . He . . . watches the grass slowly growing green beside his door." He has gained a "sense of the extraordinary freshness of life" and "a faint persistent wonder that will not leave him." He has slowed down to a pace where the calendar is more useful than the clock, and now he finds that "the coming of spring is not . . . an annual occurrence scarcely to be noticed, but an enormous personal gift that can bring tears to his eyes." It helps, on the practical side, that his wife is now busily studying for her master's degree so that she will be prepared to take up her share of the stressful breadwinner's role. The only sad thing, we are left to conclude, is that it took the agony of a heart attack to free this man, at last, to live.

Within a couple of years *Life* magazine would be devoting even greater space to denunciations of those men—"beatniks" —who would choose to let their wives work while they sat and contemplated the greening of the grass. But cardiology had already passed its own judgment on the "normal" masculine condition, and come down, without fully realizing it, on the side of the rebels.

7

FROM CONFORMITY TO "GROWTH"
The New Psychology

Gone is the *angst* of European existential analysis.
Gone too is the doubt and ambiguity of Freudian
psychoanalysis. In other words, the demons have
floated away. In their place is energy, flow, acceptance, nurture, tenderness, joy.

> Joel Kovel, describing the new psychology
> in *A Complete Guide to Therapy*, 1976

I have no extremes of feeling. I don't kill and I don't
sell out to a single marriage situation.

> Fritz Perls, in *In and Out
> of the Garbage Pail*, 1969

Starting in the fifties, psychology also began to revise its view
of men's lives and prospects. In a turnabout every bit as drastic
as medicine's reversal on gender and health, psychology discarded maturity as the universal developmental goal and introduced the doctrine of *growth*. Where the life cycle had been
seen as a quick climb leading to the plateau of maturity, there
was now an endlessly upward-curving arc. Where there had
been one turning point marked by the completion of the developmental tasks, there was now an ascending and variable se-
quence of "growth experiences," which would include, as the
new psychology grew emboldened by its own growth, not only

routine matters like intramarital adjustments, but divorce, the loss of a job and even, eventually, dying as a "growth experience."

Abraham Maslow announced the new psychology in the spirit of a scientist who had momentarily abandoned his usual caution to leak an astounding laboratory finding to the press:

> There is now emerging over the horizon a new conception of human sickness and of human health, a psychology that I find so thrilling and so full of wonderful possibilities that I yield to the temptation to present it publicly even before it is checked and confirmed, and before it can be called reliable scientific knowledge.[1]

It did not matter that there are no tests to "check" whether the human life cycle is best described as a parabola, a straight line or any other function known to mathematics. Psychology had changed its mind, or rather, those psychologists and psychiatrists who identified themselves as the "human potential movement," the "third force" or "humanistic psychology" had won out over their more reclusive and pessimistic competitors, the classical psychoanalysts. The premises of the new psychology were refreshingly upbeat: that people's impulses are basically good, that the human potential for creativity is vast, that spontaneity is preferable to stagnation and that, contrary to Freud, life is an "adventure" and not a tragedy. This was good news for anyone, man or woman, who chafed against middle-class conformity, and all the better for being delivered as if it were a late-breaking bulletin from the frontiers of science.

Maslow's scientific contribution—for he insisted that he belonged to the company of "tough-minded scientists" rather than that of "religionists, philosophers, yearners, utopians, polyannas, etc."[2]—was to open up to psychology the study of "healthy" people. Freud had gone wrong, he believed, by paying undue attention to the "sick" and neurotic patient, and this concentration had led to an unnecessarily dim view of the human condition. For his own empirical data, Maslow turned to the study of people he judged to be not only the healthiest but also in some sense the best. Problems in the methodology of selection had to be overcome, for he acknowledged that some highly creative people, like Byron, Wagner and Van Gogh, "were certainly not psychologically healthy people." With the obvious mental cases out of the way, there were still plenty of healthy creative people, and he settled on a list that included Abraham Lincoln, Thomas Jefferson, Albert Einstein, Eleanor Roosevelt, Jane Addams, William James, Spinoza, Albert Schweitzer and Aldous Huxley. Such people, in Maslow's judgment, were "self-actualizing"; not only had they mastered the routine business of living (in a way that a drifter like Van Gogh, for example, had not), but they had gone on to realize their fullest human potential. For people like these maturity was not a matter of settling down, but of strenuous ongoing actualization, moving from one "peak experience" to another, ceaselessly, into old age. If a few people could achieve the creative overdrive represented by self-actualization (SA), then why not everyone else? The task for psychology was to help the estimated 99 percent of the population who fell short of SA to grow to the fullest potential latent in their own unique and untapped "inner selves."

The eventual triumph of the Human Potential Movement, or the "Maslovian Revolution," is a matter of record. Maslow himself had been one of the first to recognize the growth potential of a psychology that addressed itself to the potential for growth in everyone, and had laid claim, as early as 1962, to "A Larger Jurisdiction for Psychology" (the title of the first section of *Toward a Psychology of Being*). As human potential therapist and Esalen functionary William Schutz put it, in his book *Joy,* "If there is one statement true of every living person it must be this: He hasn't achieved his full potential."[3] Everyone was a potential candidate for growth, and everyone was a potential winner in the therapies, encounters, exercises and guided experiences that offered, not the painful introspection of classical psychoanalysis, but "joy and more joy." It helped that the Human Potential Movement, with its emphasis on spontaneity and the goodness of impulses, echoed the hedonistic message of the consumer culture. What was no less important to its success, the new psychology offered its own critique of the consumer culture: It was right to want "something more out of life," and that "something more" could itself be purchased as one of many commoditized therapeutic experiences including, by the late sixties, Gestalt therapy, nude therapy, encounter groups, primal scream therapy and transactional analysis, plus their combinations and improved versions. At its peak, as Joel Kovel has written, the new psychology was both an industry and a kind of secular religion, enlisting hundreds of thousands of middle-class Americans in the project of self-improvement through psychological growth.[4]

The commercialism of the late-sixties Human Potential Movement, compounded by the fatuousness of its leading spokesmen, has tended to obscure what a radical departure the new psychology represented, especially at the time of its first emergence in the fifties. Historian Russell Jacoby, for example, dismisses it as "the ideology of conformism and synchronization in the era of late capitalism" and describes Maslow as a "conformist psychologist" whose idea of "liberation" was "a banal existence plus enthusiasm."[5] True enough, Maslow's model of self-actualization resembles no one so much as himself—a man whose journals record lunch expenses and faculty in-fighting in between the peak experiences of scientific insight. He did not have a sharp eye for injustice (not that the doctrinaire Freudians, who are more to Jacoby's liking, did either), and his only quarrel with big business was that its unenlightened management practices were inhibiting employee "growth." But the charge that the new psychology was "the ideology of conformism" flattens out a real and historic change. "Adjusted to what?" Maslow demanded of the truly conformist psychology which still prevailed, "To a bad culture? To a dominating parent? What shall we think of a well-adjusted slave? A well-adjusted prisoner?"[6]

If the human potential was intrinsically good and, for all practical purposes, uncharted by science, then there was no firm ground left from which to attack the deviant or nonconformist. All trajectories were possible as each unique and groping "self" reached toward fulfillment; the old end-point of "maturity" was gone, and there was no limit on growth or on the variety of forms it might assume. Maslow himself was a cautious rebel: He assumed that his self-actualizing people would, like Riesman's "autonomous" types, *choose* to observe the routine conventions even while inwardly mocking them. But in the privacy of his journal, he fretted over the tension between growth and responsibility: How far could a man go? "Very understandable," he wrote, "that people should resist acceptance of a lousy world, or a lousy family, or a lousy job, etc. . . . Now it is easy to understand that a person has to grow up into those things if they are his responsibilities; e.g., he can't abandon his wife & 6 children, he has to make a living, etc." The logical question was, "Why shouldn't he abandon this 'lousy' situation if that's what his growth requires?" But Maslow could only ask, as if to his adjustment-oriented professional peers, "Why demand that he love it?"[7]

It remained for Frederick (Fritz) Perls, who shares with Maslow the honor of being one of "the acknowledged prophets of humanistic psychology,"[8] to develop the more disruptive implications of the doctrine of growth. Perls began his career as a Freudian psychoanalyst; he had studied in Vienna under Helene Deutsch, been analyzed by Wilhelm Reich and had once, very briefly, met the master himself. As a refugee from Hitler's Germany, he had practiced psychiatry for twelve years in South Africa, observing the conventions of marriage, apartheid and the fifty-minute psychoanalytic hour. Moving to the United States in 1946, he lapsed steadily into an unprofessional bohemianism. He took up with a proto-Beat crowd that included Paul Goodman, the utopian theorist and writer, and Julian Beck and Judith Malina of the Living Theatre; he abandoned (for all practical purposes) his wife and children; and, at a time when the generation that would wage the youth rebellion of the sixties was still drinking chocolate milk, he pioneered the peak experiences offered by LSD. To Perls, the genial and ambitious Maslow was a "sugar-coated fascist"—as evidenced by Maslow's overly rigid response to having one of his lectures disrupted by the spectacle of the bearded and portly Perls crawling around the floor on his belly. (Maslow misinterpreted this simple Gestalt ploy and reportedly diagnosed his fellow prophet as "crazy.") With Perls, the psychiatrist and the Beat—last seen a chapter ago in a hostile stand-off—fuse into a single personality. He and Paul Goodman represented the Human Potential Movement at its most subversive: a combination of the sensibility of the Beat with the authority of the expert.

Their major contribution to the new psychology, *Gestalt Therapy: Excitement and Growth in the Human Personality*, co-authored by psychologist Ralph Hefferline, had little impact when it was published in 1951. Conservatively speaking, it was fifteen years ahead of its time, and belonged more in the company of R. D. Laing, who was published in the United States in the sixties, than that of H. A. Overstreet, whose book on *The Mature Mind* was a best seller in 1950. While the reading public was still ruminating over Overstreet's "maturity concept," Perls and his co-authors boldly announced that "nothing is more unfortunate than the current indiscriminate use of the words 'infantile' and 'mature' . . . 'Maturity' . . . is conceived in the interest of an unnecessarily tight adjustment to a dubiously valuable workaday society, regimented to pay its debts and duties."[9] And while better-known psychologists were enumerating the responsibilities that defined masculine adulthood, Perls, et al., wrote:

> In our times it is not the case that the average man is irresponsible, does not hold himself together; rather he is too responsible, keeps meeting the time-clock, will not give in to sickness or fatigue, pays his bills before he is sure he has food, too narrowly minds his own business, does not take a risk.[10]

Better, they wrote, that we should honor the immature and "childish" traits of spontaneity, curiosity and even "caprice."

Gestalt Therapy carried the new psychology to the verge of politics: If it was human nature to creatively experience the world through growth, then the social order should be changed. Anticipating the European "anti-psychiatry" movement of the sixties and seventies, they wrote, "adaptation to 'reality' is precisely neurosis: it is deliberate interference with organismic-self-regulation and the turning of spontaneous discharges into symptoms. Civilization so conceived is a disease." They excused Freud for favoring repression over spontaneity because he could not imagine a civilization that did not depend on repression. Perls and his co-authors could. Sounding like the Paul Goodman of the sixties, who endorsed (and to some extent inspired) the anarchic politics of the counterculture, *Gestalt Therapy* argued for a society that would "more nearly conform to a [continuing] child-heart's desire, for instance the possibility of a little more disorder, dirt, affection, absence of government, and so forth."

In his later years, as he moved closer to center stage in the burgeoning Human Potential Movement, Perls himself had little to say about the radical social possibility briefly glimpsed in *Gestalt Therapy*. If you could not change a society that demanded such a high price in individual conformity, you could still, as an individual, simply ignore the more annoying and restrictive conventions. This is what Perls had done in his own life, and this was the message of his most memorable directive: "Do your own thing." Coming at a time of national prosperity, and coming from a man who had escaped from Hitler as well as the bondage of marriage and a conventional career, Perls's prescription sounded not only appealing, but almost feasible.

But if it sanctioned nonconformity, the new psychology at the same time lost interest in conformity as an issue. Even Maslow's tempered criticisms of "adjustment" were lost in a psychology that could equally well endorse revolution or a lifetime of acquiescence, depending on which was your own, authentic "thing." In this sense the Human Potential Movement was, on the face of it, more neutral and more "scientific" than the adjustment-oriented psychology it replaced. It did not insist that the social order was worth conforming to, nor did it suggest that overthrowing the social order would be a worthwhile project for the seeker of growth. (Of course, the assumption that it is possible for everyone to accomplish their own thing without endangering their livelihood or nutritional status implies a fairly benevolent view of the status quo, as radical critics of the Human Potential Movement have often pointed out.) The critique of "conformity" implied, however vaguely, that there were institutional constraints to personal expression, actualization or growth; the new psychology resolved these constraints into individual obligations ("should feelings") such as might arise between two people sharing a room during a marathon encounter weekend. Marriage as an institution was not a problem, but one's particular spouse might be. Work in the service of corporate profit was not an inherently questionable use of time (as Paul Goodman saw it), but any particular person might have the wrong job. Such mismatches were bound to arise as each person followed his or her growth impulses, and that was O.K., because, as Perls explained in a poetic summary, that could be found, briefly, on everything from coffee mugs to needlepoint wall hangings:

> I do my thing, and you do your thing.
> I am not in this world to live up to your expectations
> And you are not in this world to live up to mine.
> You are you, and I am I,
> And if by chance we find each other, it's beautiful.
> If not, it can't be helped.

Needless to say, the one institution that the new psychology *did* threaten—at first only implicitly and more openly over time—was marriage. The male rebels of the fifties had found marriage financially burdensome and sexually repressive; the new psychologists found it, from a scientific point of view, improbable. If each person was following his or her own growth curves, the probability that two people's trajectories would overlap or run in parallel was about as remote as the chance of two meteors coming into orbital alignment. "In the path to emotional growth," wrote human potential psychologists George Bach and Herb Goldberg, ". . . each individual becomes a lonely hunter, making his way through uncharted territory."[11] Growth could easily be thwarted by "existing relationships and interactions," they continued in a language appropriate to astral forces and configurations. "When one spouse, for example, makes a significant shift in the direction of expressing real feelings and deeply felt needs, the other spouse is pressured to change if he or she wishes to maintain a workable balance. If he or she remains the same, the relationship is bound to deteriorate significantly." Psychologists had always seen marriage as "work"; the doctrine of growth transformed it into a navigational feat that would have challenged a ballistics expert. If by chance two people met for more than a brief encounter, it was not only "beautiful," but against all statistical odds.

For all the risks to "existing relationships," the new psychology ruled that the safe alternative, nongrowth, was impermissible. Maslow had identified growth with health and cautioned that any capacity left undeveloped "can become a disease center or else atrophy." Those who followed him in the Human Potential Movement saw the growth impulse as so powerful and compelling that it could only be resisted by willful repression. Thus, to deny growth was worse than lazy, it was a perverse and destructive expenditure of energy in the service of an obsolete emotion—guilt. In the popular psychology books that poured out of the Human Potential Movement in the early seventies, the potential for growth became the imperative to grow, and the reader was invited to compare his or her post-pediatric growth curve with those of more exciting or successful personalities, such as the author's. (Bach and Goldberg ended their book *Creative Aggression* with individual testimonials on the importance of personal growth to their own careers.) In *Feel Free* (*How to Do Everything You Want Without Feeling Guilty*), pop-psychiatrist David Viscott fairly hectors his readers into entering a new growth spurt:

> The chances are . . . you'll stay in the same situation, in the same role, in spite of how much you hate it. You'll stay married to the same person, no matter how many reasons you can give for leaving. You'll put off all the things you really want to do. . . . Why is it that you haven't grown out of it? Why is it that much of the time

you aren't really doing what you want, aren't really happy where you are or whom you are with [*sic*]? What's holding *you* back?[12]

Divorce, then, no longer signaled a "failed marriage" but an accomplished growth opportunity, a "passage" successfully navigated along the broad course of personal growth. Approached with gusto, it became "creative divorce," as therapist Mel Krantzler told his readers, and this was "essentially the beginning of a journey of self-discovery and development . . . that can go on for as long as you live."[13]

The new psychology was egalitarian in its application to the two sexes. Once the lid was off the life cycle, so to speak, anything was possible for women as well as men, at least in principle. Maturity, for women, had meant marriage and motherhood; growth could mean nonmarriage, a career, sexual exploration. When Betty Friedan wrote *The Feminine Mystique* in 1963, she used Abraham Maslow as her expert witness against the neo-Freudian advocates of female domesticity. After citing Maslow's view of growth as "one of the defining characteristics of human health," she asked, "What happens if human growth is considered antagonistic to femininity, to fulfillment as a woman, to woman's sexuality?" The answer was that women would be not only unhappy, which is how Friedan found them in her interviews, but that they would be, in a deeper, psychological sense, *unhealthy*.

For men, the new psychology reinforced and complemented the message from cardiology. Men knew that they would have to change, now they knew that they *could* change, and in a direction that was upbeat, expansive and fulfilling. Medicine said "be careful," and the new psychology said "take risks," but the prescriptions were the same when applied to the tasks and responsibilities that had defined masculine maturity. Medicine, in its popularized versions, ruled that these tasks were hazardous to the heart; psychology added that they were crippling to the spirit. "Responsibility" had been reclassified under "guilt" by the psychologists, under "risk factors" by the physicians. If there was an alternative to an early death, it was, by implication, a life of perpetual growth—growth pursued for its own sake and, if necessary, in defiance of all past norms for masculine behavior.

8

THE ANDROGYNOUS DRIFT

Counterculture versus
Masculine Culture

> Older people are inclined to think of work, injustice
> and war, and of the bitter frustrations of life, as the
> human condition . . . But to those who have glimpsed
> the promised land, the prospect of a dreary corporate
> job, or a ranch-house life, or a miserable death in war
> is utterly intolerable.
> —Charles Reich, in *The Greening of America*

The sixties, according to popular wisdom, changed everything.
There was the black movement, the anti-war movement, the
counterculture, the feminist movement and, not least of all, the
quiet movement of women out of their homes and into the
work force. Poorer women had always worked, or tried to
work, for money. Now they were joined by the wives and
educated daughters of the middle class. Pushed by the rising
cost (and standard) of living, and pulled by the expansion in
clerical and service jobs understood to be "women's work,"
women began entering the work force at the rate of approximately one million per year. The change meant that the old
financial pact between the sexes could, at the very least, be
renegotiated, and this time it was women who saw the possibility first. As Gloria Steinem put it, adding medical self-in-

terest to moral suasion, men should support women's struggle
for equality and independence because they "have nothing to
lose but their coronaries."

To an earlier generation of male rebels, nothing could have
seemed more perverse, misguided or—worse—redundant, than
a feminist revival. The popular masculine wisdom of the fifties
was that women had already won, not just the ballot, but the
budget and most of the gross national product. Homemaking
was a leisure activity reserved for the more powerful sex, while
a proletariat of husbands labored thanklessly to pay the bills.
Yet this smirking assessment of women's power and place con-
tributed to the feminist revival even as it declared feminism
unnecessary. Since the nineteenth century, America's official
reverence for women as wives and mothers has been matched
by an equal weight of contempt (revealed, for example, by
the failure of Social Security to recognize homemaking as labor
deserving of compensation in old age). The fifties' literature
of male protest brought the contempt into the open. Most
women were numbed by the mixed message: If you didn't grow
up to be a full-time housewife, you were a failure; if you did,
you were a parasite and a fool. Betty Friedan's groundbreaking
book, *The Feminine Mystique,* simply rubbed the message in,
and recommended "failure" (in the eyes of the psychoanalysts)
over folly, in the eyes of men.

The feminist promise to men was laid out clearly enough in
1963 in *The Feminine Mystique.* Friedan shared the prevailing
male contempt for women's domestic efforts. She described
housework as a form, more or less, of indoor loitering. Most
housework, she suggested, could be adequately performed by
"feeble-minded girls," or by eight-year-old children.[1] To pass
the time, intelligent women were forced to take up gourmet
cooking, The League of Women Voters or a pernicious involvement in their children's lives. Yet the housewives she described were not the carefree idlers so despised by *Playboy;*
who spent their days waiting lasciviously for a tryst with the
furnace repair man. What made Friedan's book a best seller
was her detailed and sympathetic documentation of the malaise

of the middle-class housewife, a woman who had been educated to expect, if not a career, at least something more challenging than the search for a matching mitten. "The road from Freud to Frigidaire, from Sophocles to Spock," Friedan quoted a contemporary newspaper article, "has turned out to be a bumpy one." Those who could not sublimate their energies into casserole recipes or their children's grade school careers fell into a torpor, turned into shrews, sought help from tranquilizers or developed the elusive psychosomatic symptoms of what Friedan called "the problem without a name," from low-grade narcolepsy and overeating to "great bleeding blisters that break out on their hands and arms."

Friedan did not rest her case on the sufferings of women, which, she knew, could easily be ridiculed as a delayed adaptation to excessive affluence. If anything, she expressed more alarm about the noxious effects of dependent and "infantile" housewives on those around them. The American housewife was a "Typhoid Mary" whose misdirected energies were a toxin spreading outward through the family to the nation. The children were the most directly affected, and Friedan described the youth of the early sixties as anomic, listless and lacking in any autonomous sense of identity. Teenage promiscuity, the defection of young GI's in Korean prisoner-of-war camps, and the "murky smog" of male homosexuality spreading across the country were all manifestations of the "progressive dehumanization" festering in the home of the American housewife. Husbands in particular suffered from the housewife's thwarted growth. They were forced to provide the status a woman could not win for herself and then—at the end of the day—to meet the exaggerated sexual expectations she had nurtured in boredom while he toiled in the adult world. (On the subject of housewives' romantic fantasies, Friedan quoted *The Exurbanites,* whose author, A. C. Spectorsky, had gone on, in 1956, to edit *Playboy.*) Citing women's impossible demands on their husbands, she asked:

> Could this be the reason for the rising tide of resentment among the new young husbands at the girls whose only

ambition was to be their wives? The old hostility against domineering "moms" and aggressive career girls may, in the long run, pale before the new male hostility for the girls whose active pursuit of the "home career" has resulted in a new kind of domination and aggression.[2]

The rising divorce rate, Friedan argued, proved "the growing aversion and hostility that men have for the feminine millstones hanging around their necks . . ."

There was one obvious solution, something that would be abundantly good for women, husbands, children: Women, at least those educated enough to chafe at domesticity and have some career alternatives, should be encouraged to get out of the house and into the work force. "I think their wasted energy," wrote Friedan, "will continue to be destructive to their husbands, to their children, and to themselves until it is used in their own battle with the world." If the male rebels of the fifties hadn't thought of this, it was, they would have said, because they believed that women would have to be dragged, kicking and biting, to get them out of their cushy suburban seraglios and into the work world. But here was a woman saying it, and to the evident appreciation of millions of other American women, including the readers of *McCall's* and *The Ladies' Home Journal,* which reprinted sections of *The Feminine Mystique* in 1963. Men would have to be fools, or blind traditionalists, not to see the opportunity. Juxtaposing an allusion to men's coronary fragility to her military metaphor for employment, Friedan held out the possibility that "perhaps men will live longer in America when women carry more of the burden of the battle with the world, instead of being a burden themselves."

Friedan can be forgiven for making it sound too simple—as if all that was required for the "next step in human evolution," as she called it, was for housewives to snap out of their stupors and husbands to step aside while the women marched out the door. She underestimated the difficulties even her educated upper-middle-class sample of women would have in finding satisfying white-collar careers. In "the battle with the world" women were, and are still, more likely to be recruited as privates than lieutenants. Equally important, she underestimated men's attachment to the privileges they accrued from the sexual division of labor between housewives and breadwinners—an error that would be amply corrected by the feminists who succeeded her in the late sixties and seventies. At the time Friedan wrote *The Feminine Mystique,* men may have been grumbling about their obligation to pay alimony for ex-wives, charge-account bills for resident wives, plus life insurance premiums for prospective widows, but these burdens still conferred a privileged status unknown to the unemployed or underpaid. The notions of success, masculinity and being a good (i.e., sole) provider were still too tightly intertwined for men to give up the last without compromising the first two. For anyone so tempted, the cautionary example of the Beats was still vivid—men who had freed themselves from their burdens only to be labeled failures and faggots. Before men in any significant numbers could heed Friedan's promise and declare themselves for women's—and men's—liberation they would have to decide that the pleasures of being truly masculine were not worth the obligations of being the breadwinner. Masculinity itself would have to lose status.

The Decline of Anti-Communist Machismo

Ever since the Second World War, the Communist threat had stood guard, in the national conscience, against the feminizing effects of the consumer culture. As long as there were Communists anywhere, there would have to be real men in America, from Joe McCarthy, who blustered that he'd like to "teach patriotism to little Ad-lie [Democratic presidential candidate Adlai Stevenson]" with a baseball bat,[8] to the urbane, but no less belligerent John F. Kennedy. Communism kept masculine toughness in style long after it became obsolete in the corporate world and the consumer marketplace. In one of

Mickey Spillane's novels, the detective-hero Mike Hammer boasted:

> I killed more people tonight than I have fingers on my hands. I shot them in cold blood and enjoyed every minute of it . . . They were Communists . . . They were red sons-of-bitches who should have died long ago . . . They never thought there were people like me in this country. They figured us all to be soft as horse manure and just as stupid.[4]

Communism demanded ideological vigilance, crew-cuts, and a talent for rigid self-control. It guaranteed John Wayne's popularity for three decades, and kept James Bond busy for a dozen films, fighting either the Russians or their surrogate seekers after world dominion. (Only in the softer seventies did the Bond films evolve from adventure to parody.)

It was as if the cold, judgmental figure of the Communist had stepped in to fill the void once occupied by the American superego. Riesman had described the decline of "inner-direction" with the transition to an affluent, consumerist society. Compared to America's easy-going, other-directed males, the Communists were formidable foes. They lived in colorless, preconsumerist austerity, where, rather than the men being "feminized," the women were masculinized—chunky, muscular and deprived of lipstick. Images of toiling Russians were presented, periodically, in the pages of *Look* and *Life* as a reminder that it was possible for Americans to be *too* soft, too suggestible, too submerged in the comforts of private life. Even Hugh Hefner, the apostle of male sybaritism, paid his due to the collective superego when he offered, in defense of *Playboy,* the argument that the magazine would not weaken America, but would help "put the United States back in the position of unquestioned world leadership," by giving men exciting new incentives to earn money.

Then, of course, we met the Communists in person. A total of 2.8 million Americans fought in Vietnam and perhaps a hundred million more watched the war on television. Here was the enemy against whom American men had measured their masculinity for twenty years of cold war, and the enemy turned out to be women, the thinnest of youths, old men and children. I once talked to a Vietnam veteran who wanted me to understand how tough the war was. It was so tough, he said, that his best buddy had to kill an eight-year-old boy. Otherwise the boy, who had a grenade, could have killed them. After he said this, he watched me testily, waiting for a judgment. Either this act proved his buddy's manhood or annihilated it. I asked what his friend was doing now, back home. The answer came out in pieces. He had an O.K. job now, two children of his own, and screaming nightmares. This was a new kind of veteran. The Second World War had produced a generation of men whose memories of masculine adventure made them chafe at post-war civilian "conformity." Vietnam produced men like my acquaintance's friend or like Wayne Felde, whose hallucinatory flashbacks to the war led to his fatal shooting of a policeman in 1978, or like the young soldier described by correspondent Michael Herr:

> He had one of those faces, I saw that face at least a thousand times at a hundred bases and camps, all the youth sucked out of the eyes, the color drawn from the skin, cold white lips . . . Life had made him old, he'd live it out old. . . .[5]

The war discredited American foreign policy even in the eyes of our Western allies; within America, it discredited the style of aggressive masculinity kept fervently alive by two decades of Cold War anticommunism. (The one great piece of popular wisdom to come out of the war experience was Pogo's aphorism—long since lost to wisdom as cliché—that we had met the enemy, and they were us.) There was no accounting for the gratuitous brutality of American fighting men, as shown in full color on television and in the pages of *Life:* the babies bayonetted at My Lai, the peasants' huts ignited with an officer's cigarette lighter, pregnant women cut open with machetes, the sexual torture of suspected Vietcong. Nor was there any entirely rational accounting for the war itself; some larger end to cover for the atrocious means. Norman Mailer's novel *Why Are We in Vietnam?* was about the aimless violence of a hunting trip, and for some young men coming of age in the 1960s, this seemed to be as good an answer as any.

Marc Feigen Fasteau traced his first "embryonic awareness of the masculine stereotype" to Vietnam. As a young Senate aide, he had scoured the Pentagon Papers and buttonholed top administration officials to find some convincing rationale for the war, but the only appeal to realpolitik—the domino theory —seemed to collapse at close range. Left with "this incredible lacuna" in the fabric of official theory, Fasteau was forced to consider "other, not fully conscious, motivations."[6] There was, for example, John F. Kennedy's intense personal competitiveness, Nixon's cult of toughness, the repeated presidential fears of "the humiliation of defeat," and Lyndon Johnson's lewd military imagery: "I didn't just screw Ho Chi Minh," he told a reporter after the bombing of North Vietnam in 1965, "I cut his pecker off." If there was no imperial calculus to explain the strategic significance of Vietnam and the drawn-out presidential obsession with victory, then Fasteau's psychohistory of the war made sense. Some masculine demiurge, latent perhaps in all men, had simply run amok.

Errant masculinity explained the war, and the war, in turn, helped discredit masculinity in its less lethal expressions. In his rambling, ambivalent introspections *On Men and Manhood,* Leonard Kriegel complained that the men of his generation, "too young to have fought in World War II and disillusioned by the limitations of all wars fought after that," had been "caught up short by their own myths" and found that "manhood, once a prize to be wrested from life, is now viewed as an embarrassment, an encumbrance to living successfully."[7]

The Counterculture and the Androgynous Vision

But the "dark days of the Vietnam war"—as the media later called them (appropriating to America even the tragedy of the Vietnamese)—were also, at least on this side of the Pacific, the "age of Aquarius," of drugs, sex, rock and roll, and a vision of expanding consumer possibilities. The counterculture of the sixties was—in some ways—the Beat revolt all over again, re-run in Technicolor and with a cast, this time of hundreds of thousands. Like the Beats, the hippies held out to men the possibility of perfect freedom from material obligations. A 1967 manifesto issued by the "Mutants' Commune" in California attacked the traditional male responsibilities with a directness that even Kerouac would have found unseemly:

> The 1919 007 betty crocker miss clairol family institution is a death form. Marriage, responsibility for children, alimony are death. Let's do away with the meaningless, unnecessary bullshit of "I want my kids to have more than I had," "My kids will starve," "I don't have time to listen to your abstract ideas, I have to support my family."[8]

But the counterculture was not a male rebellion, and not simply because the "chicks" were so numerous and so visibly rapping, tripping and dancing along with their male counterparts. The Beats had idealized defiant masculinity; the hippies discarded masculinity as a useful category for expression. If the hippie demimonde was not exactly an egalitarian one, it was, at least superficially, an androgynous one. The most shocking feature of the hippies, second only to their presumed abstinence from bathing, was that, that with all the long hair, beads and flowing makeshift costumes, "you couldn't tell the boys from the girls."

Tuli Kupferberg, a well-known countercultural poet and musician who was old enough to recall the Beat progenitors, described the change from "hip" to "hippy" as a change from "hard" to "soft," from the "tough leather" of motorcycle jackets "towards nudity," from boots to bare feet. "Boots are elegant and they ARE masculine," he wrote, but masculinity was now suspect; "The damned-up sadism exposes itself."[9] Of the fifties' Beat stars, the gentle and openly homosexual Allen Ginsberg made the best transition into the sixties, finally finding, in the counterculture, a mass audience for his mantras and visionary poems. Neal Cassady became a minor figure in the counterculture as a combination bus driver/guru for Ken

Kesey's band of Merry Pranksters, who had set out in 1964 to share their acid-based revelations with middle America. But according to Tom Wolfe, who recorded in the Pranksters' adventures in *The Electric Kool-Aid Acid Test,* the ex-convict and car thief from Denver never quite fit in with Kesey's New Age bohemians, and resented his macho image as the "holy primitive, the holy beast, the Denver kid." Kerouac was disgusted by the counterculture, the anti-war movement and all drugs other than his own sweet muscatel. According to his biographer Dennis McNally, an encounter with the Merry Pranksters, arranged by Cassady, ended with Kerouac's demanding of the flower children whether they were Communists.[10]

Kerouac's reaction was not too different from that of most middle-aged, middle-class Americans. There had never been such an outrageous or well-populated counterculture: Not just a few intellectuals flouting convention, as the expression goes, but an army of young people for whom the conventions—marriage, career, material success, etc.—were simply "unreal." Yet the counterculture of the sixties was, in America's own terms, a success. If the story of the Beats was of their marginalization and ridicule by the media, the story of the sixties' counterculture was its "co-optation" (as predicted and explained by one of the few radical intellectual heroes of the sixties, Herbert Marcuse). In part, the hippies were more likable, less standoffish and elite-seeming than the Beats had been. The Beat word for the un-Beat was "square," which implied a certain cognitive disadvantage, an ignorance (of jazz, hip vocabulary, etc.) that would betray the uninitiated. The equivalent hippie terms like "straight" and "uptight," suggested an emotional condition which could, presumably, pass away like a bad mood or a fading hallucination. Drug culture inspired a diffuse amiability in outlook as well as affect; if one's own reality could change so drastically with a hit of acid, then anyone or anything could change unexpectedly and without intervening transitional steps. In a world where a middle-aging Harvard professor named Richard Alpert could become Baba Ram Dass, personality was endlessly mutable, and everyone was potentially ready to let down their hair, drop their everyday responsibilities, and join the fun.

In addition to their intrinsic lovableness (which began to fade, however, after the Manson killings in 1969), the hippies had the advantage of stepping into a vastly different America than the Beats had inhabited. With the Communists discredited as an external enemy, liberal intellectuals could relax their guard against domestic deviance. In addition, the sudden expansion of higher education in the sixties infused the professariat—which had remained cautiously silent throughout the fifties—with new confidence to pass unfavorable judgments on the status quo. While most of them gave low grades to the counterculture (for being anti-intellectual) and to the new left (for being anti-professor), there were others, like Kenneth Kenniston and Philip Slater, whose work served as a kind of expert testimony on behalf of the young. In a somewhat different category, intellectually, there was Yale professor Charles Reich, whose 1970 book *The Greening of America* introduced thousands of grown-up middle-class Americans to the counterculture—presented as a kind of consumer paradise that anyone, including grown men, could enter.

Reich: The Voyeur in the Supermarket

Charles Reich had come of age, careerwise, in the mid-fifties —a lonely, self-conscious gray-flannel rebel. As a young lawyer in a prestigious Washington law firm, his future looked secure, if not brilliant, but he "chafed under the exhausting restraints" of his job, with its lack of "meaningful experiences" and surfeit of pressures. Marriage, with the possibility of applying his earnings to a suburban house, "silverware and expensive furniture . . . [was] something I couldn't bring myself to do."

> Marriage meant staying permanently in my present job. It meant children, a concept I was utterly unprepared for . . . It meant being "adult," which meant no more hope

of excitement, no more fun—a sudden and final leap into middle age. It would have been like a prison sentence . . .[11]

The men he encountered at work were competitive and belligerently masculine: " 'Tough-minded' was one of the highest words of praise . . . 'Hard-nosed' was another favorite." Being "tough," the young Reich realized, ruled out the sensual pleasures of consumption. In a world of consumerist temptations, masculinity meant self-denial, repression and unsatisfied appetites. In his 1976 autobiography, he described the frustrations of a typical business lunch:

> The dishes were excellent: soft-shelled crabs, imported English sole, crab meat au gratin, sliced filet of beef with a sauce. I would have liked to add an extra vegetable from the other side of the menu—asparagus hollandaise—but I held back . . . I quailed at drawing attention to the fact that I was specifically interested in the food itself . . .[12]

Once the food was served, minus the potentially embarrassing asparagus, the others would get down to business, leaving Reich alone in his appreciation of the "subtle delights of the food":

> What I really wanted, at this particular moment, was to savor the lobster bisque and the filet of sole. I would have liked to discuss the special virtues of the sauce on the filet of sole. But once the food had arrived, everyone showed a total unconcern about it. They sawed away at their filet of sole or other dishes as if they were meat and potatoes at a highway roadhouse.[18]

For the young Reich, unlike his ascetic comrades, the commodity spectacle was always a secret source of pleasure, even salvation. One night, overwhelmed by depression, he considers "a dozen remedies" and settles on a walk to the supermarket:

> I arrived at the large, modern, brightly lit supermarket, one of the prime objectives of my tour—although there was nothing I wanted to buy. I liked to walk along the rows of meats and fruits and vegetables, admiring turnips, eggplants and other things in from the farm. Heaps of

> onions and potatoes. Exotic frozen foods. The array of
> canned soups . . . Powdered mashed potatoes . . . Sliced
> almonds, to be mixed with string beans for a fancy dinner.

He leaves the store "feeling revived."[14]

Reich moved on to the more congenial profession of college teaching, and when the counterculture arrived—at Berkeley in 1967 and his own campus, Yale, a year later—he was ready to join. As preppy Yale students bloomed into hippies all around him, the fussy, middle-aged law professor was reborn as a jovial campus character (not so relaxed, however, as to neglect the nonstop note taking that led to *The Greening of America*). In the hippies Reich found friends who could articulate the precocious alienation he had felt as a young lawyer: "They saw how empty and unfulfilling middle-class life could become. They recognized that the goals of money, ambition and power were a trap." Better still, they did not find it unmanly to revel in the sensual immediacy of things; they affirmed Reich's own yen to face the world with wide-eyed, consumerist expectancy: "It was as if they had never seen anything before—trees, plants, sculpture, paintings, the sun . . . People smiled at one another all the time. They were smiling because the world was so beautiful . . . Their smiles said, 'Isn't this warm sun wonderful?' 'Don't you like the rain?' 'Look at all those great people.' 'Isn't this line at the check-cashing window ridiculous?' "[15]

In *The Greening of America* Reich celebrated the counterculture as a "revolution," and the first one to take place without violent disruption or boring polemics. His great realization was that it was no longer necessary for the middle-class, white-collar man to be voyeur in the supermarket. With a change of consciousness—and probably, clothes—he could have or at least experience, everything. Reich recognized that the old system of obligation between the sexes would dissolve as America went from chromium to green: "There is no masculinity or femininity hang-up," he observed of the hippies, nor any fidelity hang-up. "To most people, there is something frightening about the notion that no oath, no law, no promise, no indebtedness holds people together when the feeling is gone," but to hang in past the point of good feelings "is no virtue and may even be a crime . . ."[16] In case this sounded threatening, Reich enumerated all that we might expect to gain from a collective advance into "Consciousness III," the psychic stratum already inhabited by hippies and, he believed, blacks: "magic and mystery," "mind expanding drugs," "multimedia experiences," "growth, learning, change," "harmony," "responding to own needs," not to mention "bare feet."

The weekly mass magazines gave the counterculture an only slightly less effusive welcome. For one thing, it was a graphic delight after the black, white and gray tones and the obligatory male mug shots provided by the Beat underworld. Hippies were fun to look at and fun to read about, words like "tribal," "psychedelic" and "ecstatic" made the copy flow. *Look*'s early 1967 special issue on "The American Man" included "the social dropout" as an important specimen, along with the astronaut, the business school major, the GI in Vietnam, and others. *Look* editorialized enthusiastically:

> Our faceless homogenized society with its organization men, its phony Puritans, its hordes of misanthropic bureaucrats, its publish-or-perish professors is beginning to separate like milk from cream. We have the social dropout, the he-man dandy, the nonpermissive father, the dedicated soldier, the optimisic Negro, the new frontiersmen in business. There are not enough of them yet, but they share one trait. They are all uncommon men.[17]

A few months later, after a few "happenings" had established the hippies as a major phenomenon, *Time* gave them an equally up-beat cover story. Conceding that "to their deeply worried parents throughout the country, they look . . . like . . . candidates for a very sound spanking and a crash course in civics," the article offered a quick glimpse of counterculture exotica (more drugs than sex and rock and roll) and concluded wistfully:

> Indeed, it could be argued that in their independence of material possessions and their emphasis on peacefulness and honesty, hippies lead considerably more meaningful lives than the great majority of their fellow citizens.[18]

The real lure of the counterculture—and occasion for so much parental wrath—was its hedonism. In the pursuit of pleasure, hippiedom did not so much counter the mainstream culture, as anticipate it, magnify it to transcendent proportions, and enrich it. Consumer culture had always promised much more than it advertised: Not just a car, but sexual adventure; not just a pack of cigarettes, but heroic vistas and a soaring sense of freedom. The counterculture did an end run around the commodities (and with them, the dulling obligation to earn money) to the true desire: real sex, not the chromium sublimation of sex; real ecstasy, not just smoke. What the mass culture promised, the counterculture delivered—with, of course, the help of drugs, the ultimate commodity and the negation of all other commodities. Drugs could dissolve the boundary between self and object and thereby render the mere possession of things redundant. To Marshall McLuhan, as quoted in *Time,* the hippies were the keepers of the "outlawed and furtive social ideal known as the 'Land of Cockaigne,' the fairyland where all desires can be instantly gratified."

For most grown men, the hippies' fairyland looked best as a soft-porn spectacle, like the musical *Hair,* not as a real option. The counterculture did far more than the Beats had to encourage fantasies of pleasure-seeking vagrancy, but there were few recruits among adult, middle-class males. In one early seventies men's group, a former member said:

> There was a lot of talk about dropping out and not having the hassles of having to work, about the "simple life" and how spontaneous and great things could be. Some of these guys expressed envy for their teenage kids, who seemed to be really getting off and, of course, didn't have to hold down a job. But this was just talk.

Only one man known to members of the group had actually dropped out. He had left his wife and two children and an $18,000 a year job as an engineer to devote himself to bicycling and marijuana—an enviable existence, except that he now supported himself as a $4.00-an-hour laborer. For anyone too old to qualify as a "flower child" with an option to return to Mom and Dad as soon as the hippie scene palled, dropping out meant a leap from the middle class into the uncertain and possibly dangerous world below.

John Updike sent his hero Rabbit Angstrom on a sobering plunge into the counterculture in *Rabbit Redux*. Back in 1960 Rabbit (in *Rabbit Run*) could see no way out of his dreary job and appalling home life except a mad dash for the horizon. In the final scenes he took a last look at his infantile wife and his sullen, pregnant girl friend and sprinted off cross-country. When he reappears in the late sixties, in a second novel, Rabbit has stopped running and is dutifully dividing his time between his job and his television set, with an occasional drink on the way home. Then the sixties catch up with him. His wife, who has lost weight and gotten a job, turns out to be having an affair with a leftish, cosmopolitan car salesman whose anti-war views offend Rabbit almost as much as his sexual mores. When she moves out, Rabbit takes in a hippie, a lovely, lost young thing who introduces him to marijuana, vegetarian cooking and the pleasures of reading. Fellatio, which was the high point of Rabbit's sexual adventures in the first novel, becomes a bedtime routine. Rabbit starts staying home from work and staying up late to discuss politics with the young black militant who has joined the growing menage. But Updike is not as taken with the counterculture as Reich was; he has racist neighbors firebomb the house, and sends the chastened Rabbit back to work. It was a nice life, while it lasted.

Inevitably (as we knew from Marcuse) the counterculture ended by affirming the middle-class, materialistic culture it had set out to refute. Countercultural trappings made the commodity spectacle more alluring than ever, and the androgynous drift invited men to join in the fun without compromising their claims to heterosexuality. In the early seventies, retailers redid their stores as discos, complete with psychedelic sounds and light, in an effort to make shopping itself a peak experience. In men's clothing, the old austere division between business and sports clothes broke down with the coming of bell-bottomed pants, tie-dyed shirts, denim jackets and broad, outrageously colored ties. Bars brightened up with Tiffany lamps; and solicited the patronage of young, unescorted women. The undifferentiated, anesthetic martini gave way to the sensuous complexities of wine, and hard rock inspired mellow rock for the mature consumer. In the post-countercultural world of unisex consumption, men with the wherewithal to participate learned that it was not effete to be deeply interested in clothes or food or even hair styles; it was, almost certainly, attractive. Never had the consumer culture been more congenial to men, more tempting, so that if there was a time to drop out, to abandon work and the material privileges of the middle class, this was not it. Uncounted thousands of middle-class, middle-aged men—men who would have been no more inclined to drop out than to drop acid at a business lunch—underwent a safer transformation; they grew out their sideburns, wore their shirts unbottoned to display their beads or gold chains, and daydreamed (like the hero of the movie "10") of long-haired young women with exotic sexual skills.

When the women's movement arrived in full force in the early seventies, the typical—even liberal—male responses ranged from sarcasm to peevish withdrawal. The initial reports from the movement were, after all, deeply upsetting. Where Friedan had indicated a nameless system that spanned psychoanalysis, advertising and suburban architecture, the more radical of her successors blamed *men*. Where she found the "problem without a name," they popularized a whole vocabulary of male faults—sexism, male chauvinism, misogyny. Subjects that she had skirted, like the sexual division of housework and the uneven distribution of orgasms, now came to the fore as political issues. Men might be in a new mood of consumerist self-indulgence, but, they were warned, women would no longer be indulging them. No more picking up socks, punctual meal service, or cheerful acquiescence to phallocentric sex.

The hostilities aside, the new feminism still promised men relief from the burden of breadwinning. No one in the second wave of feminism argued, as most turn-of-the century feminists had, that women could hope to achieve equality while remaining in their separate sphere as the financial wards of men. Whether paid work was a means to fulfilling women's human potential, as Friedan had seen it, or as financial leverage in the battle with tyrannical males, it was a sine qua non for liberation. At the bottom line, then, men had nothing to lose but their authority over women. Gloria Steinem, the best known spokeswoman for the new feminism, made the trade-off sound relatively painless. Writing in *Time* in 1970, she said, "Men will have to give up ruling-class privileges, but in return they will no longer be the only ones to support the family, get drafted, bear the strain of power and responsibility." The article was entitled "What It Would Be Like if Women Won," and it strongly suggested that, among other things, it would be as if *men* had won too. In a feminist (or humanist) future, she promised: "No more men who are encouraged to spend a lifetime living with inferiors; with housekeepers, or dependent creatures who are still children. No more dominating wives, emasculating women, and 'Jewish mothers,' all of whom are simply human beings with all their normal ambition confined to the home."[19]

The promise of feminism—that there might be a future in which no adult person was either a "dependent creature" or an overburdened breadwinner—came at a time when the ideological supports for male conformity were already crumbling. Physicians had found men the weaker sex; psychologists were finding them perilously "rigid." The war reinforced the medical dictum that male aggressiveness was a lethal force; and the counterculture reinforced the promise, from the new psychology, of a richer life for those who could overcome their masculine hang-ups. For those men, mostly middle class, who felt the initial impact of the women's movement, feminism only upped the ante: Men learned that they would *have* to change, and in ways that often seemed unpleasant, petty or unpredictable, but in return the old financial bond between the sexes would be dissolved. And if the financial responsibilities were lightened, then men would be free to unbend, to follow the consumerist drift without dropping out and losing the perquisites of class. The seventies' combination of pop psychology and men's liberation ideology showed how.

9

THE MALE REVOLT REDEEMED

Class Uplift and Health Reform in the Seventies

> . . . a new kind of man has come to his bliss
> to end the cold war he has borne
> against his own kind flesh
> since the days of the snake.
> —Allen Ginsberg
> from "Who to Be Kind to"

In 1970, a young psychologist and former anti-war and civil rights activist named Jack Sawyer published an article "On Male Liberation" in the small, but respected, radical magazine *Liberation.* One year later, "men's lib" surfaced in *Life* magazine, which reported that the new movement had already spread from the coastal enclaves of the counterculture to Flint, Michigan, "where no one . . . can be kissed off as a longhair. Nor a radical."[1] While these stirrings were in progress a New York University graduate student named Warren Farrell was having second thoughts about his academic career. As a result of feeling pressured to "rush through my Ph.D. and assume my primary breadwinning role," he failed a section of his Ph.D. exams. But this "first major failure" was so instructive that it turned out, so far at least, to be his last, for Farrell now understood "the connection between women's liberation and my own freedom." He *"needed* [his wife] to work."[2]

In his highly successful book *The Liberated Man,* Farrell offered "twenty-one specific areas in which man can benefit from what is now called women's liberation," and the list, though slightly inflated by repetition, touches on every major theme of male discontent since the 1950s. There would, of course, be freedom from the responsibility of being the sole breadwinner, so that a man would be able to "take risks on his job" without "leaving his family in the poorhouse if he is fired," or be able to "choose an interesting low-paying position rather than an unfulfilling higher-paying position." Without the element of economic dependency, relationships with women would improve dramatically:

> The basis for any marriage or living arrangement can be more genuine . . . The liberated woman can allow a man more autonomy in his personal life . . .

Women would be off men's backs, but, Farrell assured his readers, they would still be available in other anatomical conjunctions, because "sexual interest heightens in an unstereotyped relationship" and even the sexual activities become "varied and unstereotyped." The pressures to be monogamous would also relax, or so he deduced from the feminist demand "not to be considered a sexual possession." (In this area, Farrell was careful to free women first, though the language hints that the real gain might be men's. Demanding monogamy from a woman, he said, was a way of "castrating" her feelings.) Finally, if things did not work out, marriages and other relationships would be easier to sever without a man's suffering "guilt feelings of 'leaving her with nothing' when she has 'given her best years to him.'"

Men's liberation was in part a sincere attempt to respond to feminism. But it was also the old male revolt in a new disguise —enriched by the insights of the Human Potential Movement and blessed, if offhandedly, by the approval of feminism. The male rebels of the seventies, whether or not they felt themselves to be members of a men's liberation "movement," could articulate all the old grievances and resentments, but in a way that no longer sounded spiteful or misogynist. Male self-interest could now be presented as healthy and uplifting; the break from the breadwinner role could be seen as a program of liberal middle-class reform. Every tract, article, speech and book that expressed the new male self-interest rested its case on the cardiological and emotional damage inflicted by men's traditional responsibilities; as if men's very survival as a sex were at stake. To human potential psychologist Herb Goldberg, who became a leading spokesman for men's liberation in the seventies, almost every statistical distinction between the sexes provided evidence of men's fatal burden of oppression:

> Women attempt suicide four times more often than men, but men succeed at suicide three times more often than women. Men go to doctors 25 percent fewer times than women, but when men land in the hospital, they tend to stay 15 percent longer. . . . And how come men outnumber women in prison 25 to 1? That number is so outrageous that it leads me to believe there is sex discrimination within the system.[8]

It seemed to Goldberg that "on the deepest archetypal level" the feminist movement was not inspired by women's oppression (as it may have seemed on more superficial levels) but by "the decay and demise of the male," succumbing at last under his "many onerous burdens." Masculine privilege was "a myth" and guilt toward women was "one trap from which the liberated man *must* free himself."[4]

The Demographics of Male Freedom

In fact, during the seventies, it was probably easier for men to "free themselves" than at any time since the California gold rush of 1849. In their exhaustive comparison of American attitudes in 1957 and 1976, Joseph Veroff, Elizabeth Douvan and Richard Kulka reported that the most dramatic change they observed was in "men and women's increased tolerance of people who reject marriage as a way of life."[5] In 1957, 53 percent of the American public believed that unmarried people were "sick," "immoral" or "neurotic" and only 37 percent viewed them "neutrally." By 1976, Veroff and his associates found that only 33 percent had negative attitudes toward the unmarried; 51 percent viewed them neutrally, and 15 percent even looked approvingly on people who remain single. The young Philip Roth, who complained in the fifties that men were harassed into marriage, would have been perfectly comfortable in the seventies, when an entire "singles" industry—bars, spas, vacation clubs, convivial forms of therapy—had grown up to serve those now viewed as independent or adventurous enough to avoid marriage.

In the same period of time, the image of divorce was upgraded from a grave personal stigma to, in Veroff et al.'s phrase, "a viable alternative." The divorce rate, which had been inching upward throughout the twentieth century, suddenly doubled in the decade between the mid-sixties and the mid-seventies. Unfortunately, there are no studies that can tell us who is more likely to initiate divorce—the husband or wife—and how this might be changing.* The fact that most divorces are awarded to women (and have been throughout the century) says nothing about who actually initiates the breakup, nor, of course, about whose behavior may have inspired one spouse to initiate the breakup. There is evidence that the likelihood of divorce increases with the wife's earning power, and this is often taken to mean that women have gotten "too independent." But it is also true that the more a woman earns or expects to earn, the easier it is for a man to leave with a clear conscience. As Herb Goldberg advises men, "Support your wife's assertiveness during marriage, her educational and occupational development,

---

* There is one relevant study from Florida, and I thank Joan Huber of the University of Illinois for pointing it out to me. According to this study, the liberalization of the state's divorce law in 1971 produced a gender reversal with regard to who initiates divorce proceedings. Before the law was liberalized, 62 percent of those petitioning for divorce had been women; afterward, 64 percent were men (B. G. Gunter, "Notes on Divorce Filing as Role Behavior," *Journal of Marriage and the Family*, Vol. 39, 1977, p. 95). This suggests a disproportionate interest in divorce on the part of men, at least in the state of Florida.

and anything else that will make her an autonomous, independent person. Then, during divorce it [*sic*] will make you less vulnerable to guilt."[6]

Whichever spouse initiates divorce—and despite the long-standing male perception of a female bias in divorce settlements—it is the man who is still likely to come out financially ahead. In 80 percent of the divorces where children are involved, the children remain with their mothers, yet child support, even among the middle class, is inadequate or nonexistent. And, according to population expert Andrew Hacker, despite the much-hailed mini-trend of single-father-headed households, the number of men raising children on their own actually declined in the decade of the seventies.[7] The result of divorce, in an overwhelming number of cases, is that men become singles and women become single mothers.

In fact, one of the most striking changes of the seventies was in the number of men who could literally count themselves "free." The number of men living alone rose from 3.5 million at the beginning of the decade to 6.8 million at the end.[8] (There are more women living alone too, but their number has increased only half as fast as men's. One reason for this asymmetry between the sexes is that single women are far more likely to live with children than are single men.) Of the swelling number of men living alone, almost two thirds are in the "never-married" category, and according to Veroff et al.'s surveys, 70 percent of such men view marriage negatively, as "restrictive." Impressionistic evidence from the front lines of the contemporary singles scene suggests that single, middle-class men are more elusive than ever. Women's magazines carry articles on male "commitmentphobia," and perhaps the most commonly voiced fear among single women in their thirties is that they will never meet a man whose affections are durable enough to survive the mention of pregnancy. Sociologist Cynthia Epstein speculates, in an interview with Betty Friedan, that men "figure that with a woman, even if she's working, sooner or later she's going to want to have a baby, and there goes the good life they want. They aren't about to risk becoming economic drones."[9]

"Mask-ulinity": Discovery of the "Male Role"

Yet there was, in the ideology of men's liberation, no male "revolt" in the seventies. Men were only changing, not revolting, and the changes were understood by their partisans as internal, individual and therapeutic.† As Herb Goldberg explained, "Women's movement issues are power issues, while male issues are human issues,"[10] implying that men's concerns belonged to the domain of psychology rather than politics or public policy. In practice, both men's liberation and the human potential movement as it applied to men (for brevity, I will refer to their common ideology as that of "men's liberation") invited men to claim new sexual and financial freedoms. In theory, they promoted a kind of psychological transformation, which, from the standpoint of traditional masculine values, looked more like surrender than revolt.

What men stood to gain was obvious: what they had to give up was the constellation of attitudes, habits and gestures that had for so long defined adult masculinity. In the ideology of men's liberation, this was not a trade-off, but a double gain. The prospect of shedding masculine traits no longer had the

† This generalization does not do justice to the internal politics of the men's liberation movement. I am indebted to Joe Interrante for an article in *Radical America* ("Dancing Along the Precipice: The Men's Movement in the 80s," Vol. 15, No. 5, Sept.–Oct., 1981) and personal communications explaining the tensions and divisions within the men's movement. There have been divisions since the early seventies between men who believed that their primary mission was to provide support for the feminist and gay movements, and those who emphasized men's (typically heterosexual men's) self-interest. In 1982 this division developed into factional polarization, with the more militantly self-interested group even developing a growing hostility to feminism ("Now's the Time for All Good Men to Aid Themselves," *Washington Post,* February 7, 1982). If I have slighted the institutional history of the men's movement, it is because my interest here is in the notion of male psychological transformation which grew out of the human potential movement, was promoted by men's liberationists in the mid-70s, and entered into popular culture in the late seventies.

fearful surgical implications it might have had even a decade earlier, when "castration" still stood as a general metaphor for men's oppression. If masculinity was burdensome, it was also detachable; the authentic self could set aside the "image." Men's liberationists invented new vocabularies to distance the male self from the complex of male traits: For Farrell, there was a "masculine mystique" hanging over men, like an aura of nagging expectations. Marc Feigen Fasteau discovered a robot doppelgänger, "the male machine" marching at men's sides:

> He has armor-plating that is virtually impregnable. His circuits are never scrambled or overrun by irrelevant personal signals. He dominates and outperforms his fellows, although without excessive flashing of lights or clashing of gears.[11]

To psychologist Goldberg, masculinity was a "harness," a "machine" and a "defensive operation" of the psyche. Others pointed out that the word betrayed its own inauthenticity: *mask*-ulinity.

Sociology provided a scientific vocabulary for men's alienated condition: They were playing a *role,* and in the seventies this term had acquired a theatrical sense unintended by the framers of mid-century functional sociology. Feminists had begun, in the late sixties, to speak of the "female sex role" as something distinct from the spontaneous inclinations of women, thereby raising the question, as sociologist Robert Brannon put it: "Might there not be a 'male sex role'; a distinctly male, as opposed to general human, way of thinking and acting; a male blueprint composed of culturally encouraged goals, needs and secret insecurities?"[12]

If so, it was somewhat more difficult to pin down than the female counterpart. Women's "role" was a single definite occupation, that of housewife and mother, which women of all classes (excepting the most deprived or indulged) were expected to undertake. Men, of course, have many occupations; a fact that had led the early twentieth-century psychologist G. Stanley Hall to surmise that the fundamental difference between the sexes lay in the contrast between the sameness of females and the remarkable variegation of males. In a 1976 essay, which aimed to bring together the insights of men's liberation with the rigor of sociology, Robert Brannon briefly wondered if any "common image" could unite such "diverse symbols" as Malcolm X, James Bond, Lou Gehrig, Father Berrigan, I. F. Stone, John Foster Dulles and others in a list of representative males. Intuition insisted they had more in common than met the eye: "I have gradually come to realize that I, with every other man I know, have been limited and diverted from whatever our real potential might have been by the prefabricated mold of the male sex role." A host of male discontents—coming from men of widely different classes and occupations—could easily be explained by the "scientific concept of role":

> The term *role* was first borrowed by social scientists from
> the language of the theatre . . . and much of its scientific
> meaning is suggested by the theatrical analogy.[13]

Thus, although men did not act in any way the same (or at least, no more similarly than Father Berrigan and John Foster Dulles), they were nonetheless acting. And, thanks to sociology, the theatrical metaphor had a ring of scientific finality.

Radical feminists had an alternative explanation of the common behavior that made men "masculine." If there was any similarity of gesture between a pacifist priest and the Secretary of State, it arose from the habit of command which all men exercise over women. In the radical feminist argument, the notion of sex roles obscured the power relationship between the sexes, or made it appear to be a kind of neutral specialization, like the difference between linguists and engineers, pediatricians and podiatrists. One might as well talk, as feminist Carol Ehrlich suggested, of slave "roles" and slave-owner "roles," boss roles and worker roles.[14] But this was a minority opinion even within feminism, and had little effect on the popularity of the notion of a universal male sex role. Hardliners, like Herb Goldberg, were unimpressed by men's alleged power over the women for whom they toiled, as breadwinners, to support. Others, more sympathetic to radical feminism, were even willing to incorporate dominance into the male sex role, so long as the real power still lay with the unseen author of the scripts. "Sex-role stereotypes say that men should be dominant," wrote Jack Sawyer in his 1970 essay "On Male Liberation." But if dominance was really a role that men were forced into, and not a choice, then dominance itself was actually a form of submission—another evidence of men's common oppression. "Being a master," he added—forgetting for a moment to distinguish between "being" and "acting like"—"has its burdens."[15]

The notion of a male role, distinct from men themselves and imposed on them to their disadvantage, spread quickly in all directions—moving upward to become an item of professional wisdom and downward to become an almost inescapable pop-psychological cliché. In medical circles, some researchers have begun to reinterpret the noxious Type A personality as a "response to the male role," rather than as a congenital character defect. In educational circles, teachers are alerted to the fact that "sex-role stereotyping is not a problem for women only." For example, an upstate New York newsletter for teachers of vocational education introduced its readers to the dangers of the male role as follows:

> The American Male—brave, courageous, and bold . . . He's the provider. He's the bedrock of the American family. He learns to repress emotions like fear, insecurity, compassion which leads to tears, and a certain kind of sensitivity allowed to be felt by women only.

The price is psychic alienation ("any man in America who denies being torn between his inner self and what the world expects of him is either a liar or very, very lucky") and the now-familiar fact that "men develop more ulcers than women and die at a younger age."[16]

Outside of professional literature, the critique of the male sex role can be found in a surprising variety of "low-brow" publications—for example, pornographic magazines. Contrary to the conviction held by some feminists that pornography is an unrelieved incitement to male sexual aggression, porn maga-

zines do not hesitate to attack the male "role" when it
threatens to inhibit male sexual inclinations, no matter how
peculiar. In the letters column of *Response,* for example,
M.J.F., a "pretty big girl" from Chicago, confides that her boy-
friend Dwight likes to be penetrated with a dildo and addressed
as "Diane." "What we do behind closed doors is all right,"
M.J.F. says a little plaintively, "but I'd like someone to take
care of me sometimes." This regressive yearning earns her a
stern chastisement from the editors:

> Psychologists and psychiatrists agree that men sometimes
> get tired of role-playing, of always acting and having to
> act the macho role and breadwinner . . . who will protect
> his beloved damsel from all manner of harm. This is obvi-
> ously what you've run into in Dwight/Diana [*sic*]—a guy
> who . . . isn't interested in "proving" what the rest of the
> world thinks of as his "masculinity" all the time . . . It
> sounds to us like you sense a deep yearning to go back in
> time and be the little girl who will always be protected,
> but is that always possible anymore?[17]

And in *Swank,* a magazine largely devoted to full-color crotch
shots, we find an even more urgent plea for men's liberation
from oppressive roles, this time on behalf of diaper fetishists—
men who take orgasmic pleasure in being diapered and changed
by dominant women:

> Even in this age of female liberation, the pressures on men
> in our society are immense—to perform, to succeed, to
> "score" with women, to hold up an image that is illusory
> and usually leads to an early demise. Who needs it? An
> ever-growing number of red-blooded males are turning on
> to the ultimate escape from such pressure: babyhood.[18]

The Transformation: Soft and Straight

The analysis that distanced men from masculinity implied
that men could transform themselves suddenly, voluntarily and

seemingly without reference to external circumstances (as from Dwight to Diane). Masks can be dropped; machines can be turned off; mystiques can be ignored, and roles can, presumably, be abandoned in mid-plot. Furthermore, the American reverence for authenticity guarantees that such a change will be seen as intrinsically worthwhile. Taking off a "mask" need not be seen as a guilty concession to feminism; just as stepping out of an onerous "role" need not be construed as a militant (or irresponsible) act of male revolt. Change that is represented as a step toward candor and naturalness can only be applauded, and this was how the male revolt of the seventies is depicted in the ideology of men's liberation. The cover of Herb Goldberg's book *The New Male* symbolizes the transformation with a knight stepping out of his armor: An empty suit of armor lies in the foreground, gray and menacing, while a naked leg (muscular enough to be male) steps out of the frame. The male role is a disposable exoskeleton from which the true self, the "human being inside the man," is invited to emerge.

The nature of the transformation advocated by men's liberation and associated therapies was invariably portrayed as a change from "hard" to "soft," from metal to flesh, and even beyond flesh to its moist excretions. Unreformed masculinity was characterized by clogged arteries, "emotional constipation," and the inability to cry. Hardness represented self-denial and a defensive fear of emotional contact, traits perpetuated by the pressure to succeed (as a breadwinner) in the competitive male world. With raised consciousness, blockage would give way to fluidity; stasis to flow. In a brief, two-page description of the liberated male, Goldberg invokes "growth," "rhythm" and "fluidity" repeatedly and in stirring combinations. The liberated male, that is, the authentic self which has been liberated, will be "fluid in his rhythm," "in contact with his own unique and individual rhythm," and able "to develop and to grow, to be total and fluid." He will reject "onerous life situations" and "guilt-oriented 'should' behavior" because they lead to a "hidden build-up of resentment," which is, of course, the unhealthful antithesis of flow. Unblocked and unclogged, he will be "variable" and even "unpredictable" as he cascades forward, driven only by his "inner promptings."[19]

There was still a question of how far the softening could go without, so to speak, losing the man in the warm emollient bathwater of therapeutic liberation. The qualities now claimed for the authentic male self—sensitivity, emotional lability, a capacity for self-indulgence, even unpredictability—were still, and despite the feminist campaign to the contrary, recognizably "feminine." How much could a man transform himself, in the name of androgynous progress, without ceasing to be, as Goldberg put it, "all male," or visibly heterosexual? Sanctions against homosexuality had always defined the outer limit of male rebellion; and although these sanctions did ease slightly in the seventies, what was perhaps more important for the male revolt was that homosexuality began to recede as a possibility inherent in most men and congeal into a condition specific to some: The gays became more visible and sorted themselves out from the straights.

Dennis Altman writes that "two quite new and connected ways of looking at homosexuality came into being in the seventies: the concept of the alternative life style and that of a gay *people* or minority."[20] (Emphasis added.) He describes the emergence of a distinct gay culture, with (on the male side anyway) not only gay bars and discos, but gay neighborhoods, publications and styles of dress. The "ethnicization" of gays was important to the cause of gay liberation. "After all," Altman observes, "murderers are not usually seen as a minority, nor tuberculosis as a life style." In the spirit of pluralism, cities such as New York and San Francisco could proclaim "gay pride weeks"—analogous to St. Patrick's Day, Black History Week, and other nods to ethnic interest groups—and liberals could add "gay rights" to the long list of social democratic desiderata without having to think for a moment of the unsettling sexual possibilities posed by same-sex love. Polls in the mid-seventies showed an increased acceptance of homosexuality, now understood in consumerist terms as a "sexual preference" or as a "life-style" defined by certain goods and leisure options. In 1973 the medical community, represented by the

American Psychiatric Association, dropped homosexuality from its list of diseases, and in other circles as well, "faggot" began to lose some of its sting as the ultimate male insult.

How well the ethnicization of homosexuality will serve the cause of sexual liberation remains to be seen. For the men who profess to being gay, it means a new feeling of collective pride, a base for political activism, networks of sociability and support. It also means a heightened vulnerability. Visibly gay men in identifiably gay milieus are easy targets for random harassment or murder. As a "people," they substitute for Jews in the hate literature of far-right groups—symbols of urban degeneracy, unearned pleasures, and defiance of all that is Christian and "natural." But for the men who do *not* profess to being gay, the conceptual ghettoization of homosexuality has had a clearly liberating effect: The social deviant—who departs from standards of masculine maturity—is no longer an automatic suspect for sexual deviance.

Before gay liberation and before the seventies' disillusionment with masculinity, male homosexuality could not be contained in any identifiable group of men. It was a diffuse possibility that haunted every man, a label that could be hurled against the man who was "irresponsible" as well as the one who was overtly "effeminate." If few heterosexuals could claim to know a "practicing" homosexual, almost everyone knew someone suspected of being a latent one, and the notion of "latency" expanded homosexuality to an almost universal male potential. Even such a champion of heterosexual masculinity as Norman Mailer admitted in 1959:

> There is probably no sensitive heterosexual alive who is not preoccupied at one time or another with his latent homosexuality, and while I had no conscious homosexual desires, I had wondered more than once if really there were not something suspicious in my intense dislike of homosexuals.[21]

But, in the seventies, when homosexuals became "gay," and gays became a "nation," "tribe" or, less bombastically, a "community," the gray areas began to vanish.‡ You were one or you were not, in much the same sense that you might be Irish or Jewish, or not. Where the notion of latency had established a secret continuum between the heterosexual and the homosexual, there was now a sharp divide, like a national boundary: Gays on one side, "straights" (as they now became by default) on the other. What this meant for the straight man was that he could indulge in a wide range of formerly suspect behavior without ever losing the privileges of heterosexual "citizenship."

It helped considerably that what became the badges of *gay* citizenship in the seventies were exactly the opposite of the clues that once signified "latency." In a curious crossover, gay trend setters preempted the "macho look" and adopted it as a uniform just as other men were accepting a new variety, texture and looseness in their appearance. Gay visibility came to mean short hair, flannel shirts, tight jeans, Levi jackets and leather boots. "It is now in straight discos that one finds the soft-looking and long-haired males," Altman observes, "gays are too busy striking masculine poses and flexing their pectorals." Homosexuality might still be feared and stigmatized, but it could no longer be used as the null point in a hypothetical scale of masculinity.

With the old equations between homosexuality and effeminacy broken, straight men were free to "soften" themselves indefinitely without losing their status as heterosexuals. The only thing to fear was the *fear* of homosexuality—not because it endangers those who are visibly homosexual, but because it limits men who are not.

‡ It is true that we now speak of "repressed homosexuals" and these have in some ways taken the place of the "latent homosexuals" of the fifties, but the implication is very different. The "latent homosexual" was seen as unwittingly disclosing his true nature while the "repressed homosexual" is believed to be *denying* his true nature, like the Jew or light-skinned black who would once have tried to "pass." The mark of the latent homosexual was the irrepressible gesture or impulse, while the mark of the repressed case is the work of repression itself. Mailer was sensitive enough to examine himself for both kinds of stigmata: the unconscious desires and the effort implied by his "intense dislike of homosexuals."

Liberation in a Hot Tub

The transformation of Dr. Richard Abell, detailed in his 1976 book *Own Your Own Life,* is striking both for the intensity of his experience and for the wealth of imagery that, as a psychiatrist, he insightfully provides. The setting for his conversion—and no doubt that of thousands of other upper-middle-class men—was Esalen, the West Coast pop psych spa and former headquarters for gestalt guru Fritz Perls. Attracted by the gestalt idea that he is "not in this world to live up to anyone's expectations," Dr. Abell arrives "with hope and misgiving." He is wearing "a gray flannel suit, stocking garters, black shoes, a white shirt, and, of course, a tie," in unsettling contrast to the first Esalen-dwellers he encounters: "Their hair was long, their shirts were open to the waist, their feet were in sandals." On the bright side, though, he has managed to lose his luggage on the trip from New York, which, he tells us, "you may interpret symbolically if you like."[22]

His clothes soon go the way of his luggage, as Dr. Abell makes his way through a heavy curriculum of body therapy, group therapy, nude bathing. Everything seems to be going well; insights are multiplying, psychic armor is beginning to crumble, and pretty young women are giving him good grades in nonverbal communication experiments. A remarkable amount of time is spent soaking in a collective bath, where Dr. Abell seems to be well on the way to liquefaction, when something happens to jerk him back into rigidity:

> Suddenly I felt someone's toes exploring my genitals. I looked up to see whose foot it was. The light was dim, and the bath was crowded, but the foot seemed to come directly from Ralph, a somewhat effeminate-looking man of about thirty.[23]

Dr. Abell is "furious" and, in the Esalen spirit of emotional openness, uses the next group therapy session to accuse Ralph publicly of the assault. But, surprisingly, Dr. Abell is ostracized by the group from that moment on; his outburst has betrayed his fear of homosexuality, his recidivist uptightness. Hurt and rejected, he heads toward an emotional crisis. (The possibility that his anger was valid, and that someone had been maliciously teasing him in the tub, is no longer entertained by Dr. Abell, who wisely recognizes the benefits of experiencing an emotional crisis while he is in residence at Esalen, no matter how it is provoked.) As soon as the group is reassembled, he desperately seeks acceptance. When he is rejected once again, he seizes the opportunity to break down completely and to achieve—after so many decades of dry-eyed adult masculinity —a good cry:

> I could feel my throat becoming tight. It seemed to be undergoing a kind of spasm quite beyond my ability to control it. It took over, and I lay down on the floor and began to cry convulsively . . . the floodgates broke. I cried, I sobbed, I lay on the floor, convulsed . . . I had let go.[24]

From the hot tub to the pool of self-pitying tears, Dr. Abell's liquefaction is complete. His fellow group members now welcome him with hugs and kisses. Dr. Abell has put aside his roles, his psychic luggage, and tells himself "I'm going to be 'me.' "

Masculinity and Class

In the macro-theory of men's liberation, the individual conversion process took its place in a larger scheme of middle-class uplift and self-definition. The counterculture had temporarily blurred class lines among men, mixing Ivy League dropouts with disillusioned Vietnam veterans, hip young professionals with unschooled street kids, and creating a set of common values that united the upward-bound with the permanently down-and-out. But, from within the counterculture, Charles Reich had discerned three levels of personal evolution

that potentially corresponded to degrees of social status and
something very like the old notion of "maturity": Consciousness I (competitive and aggressive); Consciousness II
(acquiescent to the corporate state—much like Riesman's
"other-directed" condition); and Consciousness III, the highest
level (attained to by hippies and a few prescient professors).
When theorists of men's liberation attempted to dissect the far-
from-uniform male role (and men's post-role possibilities), a
crudely parallel three-level scheme emerged. It had always
been clear that what was called the "male sex role" covered at
least two very different masculine possibilities: one physically
expressive, "macho" and overtly aggressive; the other more
like the pre-Esalen Dr. Abell—uptight, emotionally inhibited
and fastidiously devoid of affect. Robert Brannon, Warren
Farrell, Marc Fasteau and others recognized that the two types
corresponded to stages in the middle-class male life cycle. Little boys were forced to prove themselves athletically; they
learned to fight or at least to swagger. Once grown into a professional or managerial adult occupation, the male acquired
the verbal means of command and the emotional distance necessary to function in a bureaucractic setting. Warren Farrell
astutely noted the close fit between (middle class) masculinity
and the characteristics of the classic bureaucracy; as described
by Max Weber:

> Its specific nature . . . develops the more perfectly the
> more bureaucracy is "dehumanized," the more completely
> it succeeds in eliminating from official business, love,
> hatred, and all purely personal, unrational, and emotional
> elements which escape calculation.[25]

The emotions, the irrational and the possibility of being "human" were precisely what men's liberation sought to reclaim
for men. Thus, a "successful" male life cycle would proceed
through the stage of boyish physical aggression, on through
adult masculine coldness, and then, with luck or skillful therapy—on to the equivalent of Consciousness III: liberation,
fluidity, humanization.

When only adult men were considered, it was evident that

not all of them had made it to the second stage. Many of them (a majority, in fact) failed to achieve the kinds of occupations —like psychiatry or management—that required a studied, Weberian impersonality. Psychologically, they remained arrested at the boyhood level of physical expressiveness. Farrell called these "physical-strivers" to distinguish them from the "student strivers" and "leadership strivers" more commonly encountered in graduate school and the middle-class work world. All men suffered from their constant striving, but none was more pathetic than the one whose ambitions remained vested in his musculature. "Of all the strivers, the physical striver appears to suffer the most from masculine values the older he gets," since, obviously, the rewards for this type of prowess declined rapidly after the final football game of his high-school senior year. As if offering a fresh sociological observation, Farrell noted that "with the exception of the few who play sports professionally, the student and leadership strivers become the most successful job strivers."[26]

The official ideology of liberal sociology and men's liberation was egalitarian: All men were oppressed by the same stereotypes, imprisoned in the same male sex role. But within that metaphorical prison—as in any real one—the chances of rehabilitation depended markedly on one's class of origin. Men's liberation not only shared but reinforced the liberal middle-class perception of blue-collar males as culturally retrograde "hard hats." Charles Reich had called them the "arch-opponents of the new consciousness," and sex-role sociologist Joseph Pleck found them trapped in the "traditional" male role, "where interpersonal and emotional skills are relatively undeveloped," relative at least to "middle-class culture." The Weberian role of the middle-class man had its manifest limitations, but it was at least up-to-date, or, in Pleck's typology, "modern," while the working-class male role was marked by "obsolescence" and "dysfunctionality."[27]

The literature on the male sex role offers only scattered attempts to explain the perceived backwardness of blue-collar men. The most common explanation is that they are compensating in the only way they know how for the humiliations attendant on their low occupational status. Lacking power over other men, they are overbearing to women; and, lacking the substance of public authority, they have to make do with its facsimile—the make-believe authority of machismo. An alternative explanation comes from the English men's liberationist Andrew Tolson, who is the only one, as far as I know, to suggest that the working-class version of masculinity might serve some purpose other than letting off steam. He argues that the "seemingly anachronistic working-class masculinity" can help generate real power in, for example, workplace confrontations with management:

> . . . the language of masculinity contributes to a supportive, working-class culture, capable of local resistances, and even of subversion. The richness of this culture—its flexibility and spontaneity—has only recently become apparent to middle-class eyes. In this context, working-class male chauvinism . . . is a vital cultural defence.[28]

Any serious attempt to understand class differences in masculine roles would probably have to start by confronting the limitations of what is "apparent to middle-class eyes." These would include not only the possibility of class prejudice in the eye of the beholder, but the possibility that patterns of working-class behavior may be formed, in part, in response to middle-class behavior and observation. The middle-class "gaze" (in Foucault's expanded sense of observation and surveillance) can be an uncomfortable one—associated, in lower classes, with workplace supervision and with negative judgments by teachers and other authorities. What appears to be a lack of "interpersonal skills" can be a withdrawal from middle-class discourse; what looks like residual "physical aggression" can be actual and ongoing hostility; and what Tolson took to be "working-class male chauvinism," might be an expression of class, rather than gender, antagonism. An acquaintance of mine, who works in a factory warehouse, explained the kind of dynamic that can arise between blue- and white-collar men:

"We had a manager here who was always wanting to 'level' with people psychologically, but in his view I think all of us out here [the warehouse] were a bunch of animals. Well, we thought he was full of shit."

Whether the blue-collar male is actually as benighted as he seems, or perhaps has some good reason for his belligerence, is not a question that has consumed American sex-role theorists. He was assigned, in the scheme of things, to the lowest level of consciousness, the dumping ground for all the vestigial masculine traits discarded by the middle class. His association with a prior stage of the middle-class life cycle—boyish "physical striving"—only confirmed his diagnosis as a psychic retard; and, in keeping with American egalitarianism, this diagnosis substituted for more overt and now outmoded forms of class prejudice. In the seventies, this chain of associations sedimented down from the avant-garde of academically trained writers to become part of the more general middle-class culture.

Machismo in the Movies*

The movies of the seventies, for example, returned obsessively to the interlocking themes of masculinity and class, and in accordance with the sociological categorization, Hollywood located "traditional" masculinity in the working class, much as it had once been located in the filmic West. Various judgments followed, not all of them in accord with the liberal, middle-class perspective on sex roles. In *Rocky,* the muscle-bound Italian-American hero is romanticized in contrast to the cosmopolitan middle-class outer world where a cynical black man reigns as heavyweight champion. At the same time, though, the film condescends to its working-class hero, who is portrayed as a sub-conversational primitive—a baffled, but kindly "physical

* A version of this section originally appeared in "Machismo and Hollywood's Working Class," co-authored with Peter Biskind, *Socialist Review,* No. 50–51, 1980.

striver." *Breaking Away* and *Blue Collar* explored the tensions between working-class and middle-class men, and were unusual in giving most of the good lines—and some of the victories—to the former. But other films, such as *Bloodbrothers* and the highly successful *Saturday Night Fever,* offered didactic condemnations of traditional masculinity, and took their young heroes on a saga of self-improvement remarkably parallel to that offered by middle-class men's liberation.

In Robert Mulligan's *Bloodbrothers* (1979), the masculine alternatives are laid out with stark clarity: Stony De Coco (Richard Gere) can either be a "man," like his father and uncle, or he can, in the film's terms, "grow up." For career choices, Stony has to decide between following in his father's footsteps as a construction worker or defying his father to work as a children's recreation assistant in a hospital. It's a choice between two worlds. On the one side are the union and the family, on the other is the unfamiliar middle-class world of social service. The first choice offers male camaraderie and the joy of skilled, physical labor—not to mention the most stirring moments in the film's musical score. Despite these attractions and his father's opposition ("A recreation assistant? That's woman's work!"), Stony is drawn to the hospital, where we see a softer, more nurturing and creative side of his personality emerge. His girl friend, Annette, a "liberated" proto-feminist young woman, reinforces the point that "there is something more out there besides playing cool, macho and getting laid. You could even go to college, get a degree." Traditional masculinity is constrictive and dead-ended; feminization (in the film's terms) offers upward mobility.

In the end, it's not so much the attractions of the middle-class career option that tips the balance for Stony, but the horrors of blue-collar family life. His father's "traditional" masculinity, which seemed functional enough in the barroom or on the construction site, turns into uncontrollable destructive force at home. Stony's mother, a representative of the traditional housewife role, is a hysteric who has managed to induce *anorexia nervosa* in Stony's frail younger brother. When the fa-

ther catches her on the brink of infidelity, he beats her sense-
less and goes right on kicking her while she's down. With this,
Stony begins to see his family (and class) from the perspective
of the doctor who has befriended him at the hospital: His all-
too-traditional parents are deranged—little more than professional outpatients or emergency-room regulars. This was also
the diagnosis of *The Wanderers,* which featured teenage gang
members and adult mobsters as representatives of blue-collar
masculinity. The message is that the working class may be an
attractive location for masculine mayhem, but viewed "objec-
tively" by a professional (doctor or filmmaker) it is strictly
pathological. In *Bloodbrothers,* Stony grabs his little brother
and takes a cab into the night—presumably heading for the
middle class.

Saturday Night Fever passes the same judgment, but with
even fewer second thoughts. Tony Manero (John Travolta)
lives out a nocturnal male fantasy life in Bay Ridge, a mostly
Italian community trapped between the glamour of Manhattan
and the prosperity of the suburbs beyond. At home, there's not
even a towering patriarch to give zest to family life; Tony's
parents are dreary, bickering, beaten-down souls. Work—as a
clerk in a paint store—is even duller. All the music and color
in the film are reserved for Tony's leisure life as the local disco
king. Out on the dance floor, with the big beat and the pulsing
lights, he struts out a stunning pantomime of male power and
sexuality.

But, almost conscientiously, the film shows us the ugly,
"real" side of working class life in Bay Ridge. When Tony's
not working or dancing, he's gang-fighting Puerto Ricans or
gang-banging the girls on the block. In *Saturday Night Fever's*
version of working-class teen life, sex roles are tediously traditional: The young men are tough exhibitionists, and the girls
are pathetic hangers-on. The only exception is Stephanie Man-
gano (Karen Gorney), a Bay Ridge girl who's had a taste of
"culture," represented by ballet lessons, books, and an apartment in Manhattan. Like Annette in *Bloodbrothers,* Stephanie
articulates the film's critique of the dead-ended, male-dominated

working-class setting. From her point of view, Tony is good enough for an occasional fling on the dance floor, but he's too dumb to make it as a steady date.

Two incidents bring Tony around to Stephanie's judgment of Bay Ridge. First he learns that a dance contest he and Stephanie had won was rigged by the club's Italian owners to keep the prize from a Puerto Rican couple. Indignantly, he crosses the club's color line and hands the trophy over to its rightful winners. The next jolt is not so easy to handle. Tensions among Tony's rough-and-tumble buddies erupt into drunken high-jinks on the Verrazano Narrows Bridge. When a friend falls to his death, Tony realizes that machismo may be an asset on the dance floor, but it's a health hazard at high altitudes.

But Tony has one more lesson to learn. In the tradition of Bay Ridge courtship, he tries to rape Stephanie in the back seat of a car. To his surprise, she is not grateful but furious, and vanishes back to Manhattan. Bleary-eyed and repentant, Tony crosses the Brooklyn Bridge to find her and apologize. Thanks to Stephanie, his first glimpse of a "liberated" woman, he now understands that what was boyish in Brooklyn is boorish in more sophisticated boroughs. When Stephanie lets him know they will be friends, not lovers, he meekly accepts a role that would have been unthinkable only weeks earlier. The "traditional," "physical-striving" masculinity that worked well in Bay Ridge is passé in the wider world he now aspires to. What Tony will do in the big city is left unclear, since his only skills are disco dancing and selling paint. But the equation has been established between upward mobility and personal growth; Tony is invited to transform himself.

As films like these showed, the equation that linked machismo to arrested growth to the lower class could work the other way too—to de-class masculinity. If machismo was lower-class, it could be out of style—like undershirts, Vitalis or plastic furniture coverings and other saucheries. The ascent to men's liberation runs parallel to the path of upward mobility: from Consciousness I (blue collar) to Consciousness II (white collar) to Consciousness III, in which the shirt is multicolored, unbuttoned and unconfining.

The Liberated Heart

The initial and irrefutable reason for men to transform themselves was not to improve their social status or expand their souls—but to save their lives. No treatise or document of men's liberation, no matter how brief, failed to mention the bodily injuries sustained by role-abiding men, from ulcers and accidents to the most "masculine" of illnesses, coronary heart disease. In the seventies, cardiologists Meyer Friedman and Ray Rosenman, who had done so much to publicize the hazards of masculine compulsiveness a decade earlier, offered a harsh reassessment of the malignancy of the Type A personality. While they continued to deny that Type A-ness was a neurosis, it had become a "sickness" in their 1974 book *Type A Behavior and Your Heart,* and the "A-men" were now described as "afflicted" and "severely afflicted"—even in the absence of coronary heart disease. Fortunately for the victims, the doctors simultaneously revised their judgment of the intractability of Type A-ness. Type A's could become Type B's, just as occupants of Consciousness II could move to Consciousness III, macho men could become gentle and tough kids from Bay Ridge could become gentlemen.

In *Type A Behavior and Your Heart,* Friedman and Rosenman first intimidate the reader with technical descriptions of chylomicrons, beta-lipoproteins and arterial plaques, before going on to provide a purely fictional account of the transition from A to B.[29] With a bow to Sir William Osler for legitimizing the case-study approach to medicine, they present "Paul," a typical Type A, and "Ralph," a typical Type B. Paul has the well-known hallmarks of his condition: He is harried, consumed by his job, and generally unpleasant to those around him. Ralph is reflective, kindly and even a little phlegmatic. For good measure, Paul avoids exercise, breakfasts on two eggs and sometimes bacon, eats "generous" servings of meat at lunch and dinner, downs at least four martinis and smokes two packs of cigarettes a day. Ralph does not smoke, has a daily exercise routine, eats eggs "only on Sunday mornings," confines himself to a salad for lunch and often substitutes a glass of wine for his pre-dinner cocktail.

In their 1950s research, Friedman and Rosenman might have been content with this much "data." Paul displays every known risk factor for coronary heart disease (except hereditary vulnerability), plus a few unrelated bad habits (such as the martinis); and, sure enough, both his blood pressure and serum cholesterol levels are dangerously high. But the medical scrutiny continues, ranging into habits and traits that are ever further removed from the biochemistry of cholesterol. Paul is bored with his wife; she is insensitive to him; he has no real friends and he does not like his sons, with their anti-establishment views, their mode of dress and what he considers their strange unawareness of the "realities" of life. He is, in short, a pre-New Age character, out of touch with his own emotions and closed off to those around him. Ralph, on the other hand, had no difficulty "relating": He has an understanding wife, five close friends, and "no difficulty in communicating with his two married daughters, or with his son." He also has normal blood pressure and a commendably low level of serum cholesterol.

It is not enough that Paul is emotionally underdeveloped, he is also, like the unreformed Tony Manero, culturally uncouth. "He rarely visits a museum, library, or art gallery," preferring "to watch sporting events on his television set," and he seems most at ease with his social inferiors—waitresses, garage attendants and barbers. Ralph, meanwhile, boasts a long list of esthetic and intellectual avocations. He prints books ("with an antique Columbian hand press") and collects books; he loves the theater and classical music. "He finds time almost every evening to spend fifteen minutes or half an hour listening to some great piece of music," the doctors tell us (the nature of the observation betraying a certain residual Type A-ness on their part). Even Ralph's occupation is classier than Paul's: He is a bank president, while Paul, who is equally wealthy, is the manager of a brewery.

What will become of men like Paul? *"We will never, never*

believe that it is ever too late to aid such a person . . ." the
doctors vow. He must foreswear, of course, his old two-egg,
four-martini way of life, but to get at the core of his Type
A-ness, he must embark on a wide-ranging program of self-
improvement. He must upgrade all his nonwork activities and
interests, asking himself, "How many of these activities have to
do with your concern with art, literature, drama, philosophy,
history, science, and the wonders of the natural world around
you?"[30] While not explicitly proscribed, neither are lower-
class activities like bowling or playing pool recommended for
the man who aspires to clean, unclogged arteries. Improve-
ments in vocabulary can also promote the A-to-B transition:
"learn new words, expand your mind and your thinking
processes." It helps, too, to seek out Type B friends, even if
they are a little peculiar, remembering that persons possessing
"lively disease-free coronary arteries oddly do seem to be par-
tial to the more exotic and nonmercantile aspects of life in
the world." Nor should the man convalescing from Type
A-ness be afraid to indulge in nonmercantile and possibly
effeminate fancies of his own. Friedman and Rosenman offer
the example of "a rather staid-appearing banker" who secretly
fantasizes about whether flowers can dream, and if so, what
they dream about. "Admittedly, he might not be asked to stay
on several boards of directors if his colleagues were aware of
his notions." But, fortunately for this fey representative of
finance capital, these "are his own closely guarded ideas!"[31]

Even as they wrote, however, Friedman and Rosenman's
recommendations were being superseded by a more direct approach to cardiac health: Middle-class Americans, and men in
particular, were swept up by a new obsession with physical
fitness. Men who had been sluggish white-collar workers took
up jogging, health foods, racquetball and aerobic exercises—
and these activities became the new insignia of class status,
replacing less visible and indoor passions such as classical
music or rare books. Where Rosenman and Friedman prescribed upgraded cultural tastes as a means to physical health,
keeping healthy became a symbol of good taste in its own
right. The liberating project of self-transformation has come,

increasingly, to include a program of physical rehabilitation, with the new male qualities of sensitivity and self-nurture now focused on sagging muscles and suspect arteries. Popular psychotherapies offer to engage the body as strenuously as the soul: A brochure for a program called "Metamorphosis," for example, offers not only ego-analysis, Arica therapy, psychodrama and gestalt, but "psychocalisthenics," "movement," tennis, "fresh fruits and high-protein salads."

The fifties' models of male rebellion, the playboy and the Beat, were simultaneously their decade's leading exemplars of decadence. This was the image they were given and, very often, the one that they cultivated. If they were "sick" by conventional standards, they didn't care; it was part of their status as nonconformists, as marginal men. Their successors in the seventies were no longer marginal, and health, both in the sense of physical fitness and emotional growth, was a value they could claim as their own. In the seventies' cluster of middle-class male values, health was linked to class status, and both in turn were linked to a movement away from the rigidity of the breadwinner's role. With the eighties, even the consciousness of rebellion seems to have faded. Where we once had "deviants" and suspected neurotics, we now have the genial young man in the advertisement for *TV Guide* magazine: He is smiling, physically fit (riding a bicycle, in fact) and identified proudly as "27—with zero dependents."

10

BACKLASH
The Antifeminist Assault on Men

The covert female chauvinist emerges as a formidable
antagonist to the liberation and survival of the male,
since the entirety of her life style is predicated on the
maintenance of the Masculine Mystique.
—Harvey Kaye, M.D.,
  in *Male Survival: Masculinity Without Myth*, 1974

If memory serves, it was Washington Irving who said
that a true woman is serene until her den is threatened, and then she fights like a lioness to defend it.
  Now is the time for real women to roar.
—Alan Stang, in *American Opinion*, December 1969

On June 30, 1982, the Equal Rights Amendment, which would
have amended the Constitution to prohibit discrimination on
the basis of sex, was defeated. The ERA had been a major—
perhaps *the* major—goal of the American feminist movement
for ten years. It would have rendered unconstitutional dozens
of arcane state laws that limit women's property rights during
and after marriage. It would have strengthened women's position as wage earners—helping open up higher-paying, tradi-
tionally male jobs and providing a wedge against all the subtle,
informal mechanisms of wage discrimination. It would have, in
symbolic fashion, finally given women recognition as full and
equal citizens. Yet, in an irony that feminists and their liberal

supporters have yet to fully grasp, the defeat of the ERA was celebrated by its opponents, gathered 1,400-strong in the grand ballroom of Washington's Shoreham Hotel on the evening of June 30, as a "great victory for women" and as a "great achievement by women."

Most of the celebrants at this event were, in fact, women. Many were middle-aged and middle class, and seemed slightly out of place in floor-length pastel gowns that looked as though they had done prior service in decades of Rotary Club balls; others had the confident look of Sun Belt wealth, their hair frosted, skins tanned. Most of them had been foot soldiers in the campaign against the ERA, and had well-rehearsed reasons for their opposition. "Women have all the freedom they need already," said Lillian Smitherman from Winston-Salem, North Carolina, referring all further questions to her husband. "It would have desexed society," a stylish thirty-four-year-old from Baltimore told me, "There would be unisex rest rooms." Another woman, who had flown to the event from Lake Oswego, Oregon, feared that sexual equality would legitimate "homosexual marriages," and that the homosexuals, thus encouraged, would start reproducing. A retired general averred that the ERA would require women to be drafted into combat duty. Several women said they feared "the destruction of the family" and one tired-looking woman from Boston believed the ERA would lead to a state of unisex anarchy in which "the difference between the sexes would be abolished by law."

Of all the fanciful arguments used against the ERA in the ten-year campaign for its passage, the most compelling one, and the one that probably did more than any other to mobilize the female opposition, was economic: that equality would take away "the rights women already have," that is, the "right to be a housewife." When organized opposition to the ERA surfaced at the beginning of 1973, it was with the stated concern that the ERA would "abrogate the laws that require men to support their families." And, apart from the lurid possibility of encountering men over mixed-sex urinals, it was this threat that inspired the thousands of women who showed up at state capitols throughout the country to lobby against the ERA and for "the preservation of the family." A pamphlet from the anti-ERA League of Housewives, an offshoot of the multi-issue antifeminist group which called itself, cheerfully, "Happiness of Womanhood," asserted that it is

> the right of a woman to be a full-time wife and mother, and to have this right recognized by laws that obligate her husband to provide the primary financial support and a home for her and their children, both during their marriage and when she is a widow.[1]

Mrs. Jacquie Davison, the founder of Happiness of Womanhood, was proud to state that her own husband provided not only for her personal needs, but also—evidently without legal compulsion—for her organizational expenses.[2]

The fact that there are no laws requiring husbands to buy life-insurance policies did not weaken the anti-ERA forces' insistence on women's "right" to lifelong support. Nor did the fact, only slightly less accessible to the casual student of the law, that those state laws that do name the husband as the primary provider have never been enforced to win a larger share of a husband's wage for any resident wife. The "rights" and "privileges" that the antifeminists believe are accorded to women by marriage are, at best, private arrangements reinforced by convention; at worst, comforting fantasies. In neither case are they threatened by legal injunctions against sex discrimination. What was at stake in the battle over the ERA was the *legitimacy* of women's claim on men's incomes, and for this there was reason enough to fear—and to judge from the intensity of the opposition, fear enough to abandon reason.

If she read the antifeminist literature available to her, the average woman who lobbied against the ERA with offerings of home-baked bread or future votes was remarkably well-informed about at least one sociological datum, the divorce rate. If, in addition, she did some thinking about her own chances of making a living as a self-supporting wage earner (and she would have to do this thinking on her own because the antifeminist literature is studiously silent about women's collective disadvantage as wage earners), she would have formed a

terrifying sense of her own vulnerability. The slightest outward
ripple from the sexual revolution or the human potential movement could be enough to dislodge a husband from his marriage
and catapult his ex-wife into sudden, midlife downward mobility. Faced with such a possibility, a woman could, quite
sensibly, decide that the feminist promise of eventual economic
equality was so much pie in the sky. Better, perhaps, to check
the forces that allow men to think they have no natural obligation to support women, and one of these, clearly, was feminism
itself.

In the ideology of American antifeminism, it is almost impossible to separate the distrust of men from the hatred of
feminists, or to determine with certainty which is the prior impulse. There is a clear recognition that "men have rebelled," as
anti-ERA leader Kathleen Teague puts it, and sometimes an
acknowledgment that their rebellion has inspirational sources
other than feminism. "The man is not responsible anymore,"
observes Onalee McGraw, who is credited by the *Conservative Digest* with being a national pro-family leader. "It's the
whole me-decade thing . . . humanistic psychology," she explained in an early 1982 interview, "and men are taking advantage of the situation." To antifeminists who focus on the
issue of abortion, it is the possibility of sex without babies that
has undermined male responsibility. After all, if pregnancy is
"a woman's choice," as feminists insist, what's to prevent men
from thinking that it's also a woman's responsibility? In a 1980
speech offered "in defense of the Christian family," anti-abortion leader Mrs. Randy Engel presented the view that, "men
desire sex without responsibility. They become unmanly and
frightened by the thought of having to assume economic responsibility for a family: They instinctively try to escape."[8]

But the antifeminist analysis of male irresponsibility stops
short of questioning the structural insecurity of marriage. Distrust of men takes the socially more acceptable form of resentment directed at the would-be independent woman, who, in her
selfishness, would undermine other women's fragile privileges.
Thus, behind every male rebel the antifeminists can point to a
female instigator—to Mrs. Engel, it is the "emancipated, pill-

taking" wife who deprives her husband of the chastening effect
of frequent conception. Teague and McGraw blame organized
feminism. "No-fault divorce laws and cultural acceptance of
the nostrums of total sexual equality," McGraw has written,
"have liberated many men from the obligation to support their
wives and children."[4] In conversation, she is blunter: The male
rebellion has "victimized women," and "women's lib has to answer for it."

If men are rebelling in a way that hurts women, children and
even unborn babies, then the women who abet them must be
either traitors or fools. The genius of Phyllis Schlafly, chief organizer and ideologue of the anti-ERA movement, was to
argue that feminists are both. In her book *The Power of the
Positive Woman,* which is considerably milder in tone than her
public utterances, she observes that "some ERA proponents
argue that husbands support their wives only because of love,
not because of the law." This, she quickly explains, is foolish
romanticism, because love "is not apt to survive all those years
'for better or worse, for richer for poorer, in sickness and in
health, till death we do part.'" Love is one thing; duty is another, and "duty is essential to marriage." "Furthermore," she
warns, "the high divorce rate proves that many husbands have
stopped loving their wives."[5] If men have become less willing
to volunteer their support, then it is hardly the time to relax
the external constraints on them. "Should a husband have the
legal right to stop supporting his faithful wife of twenty or
thirty years by the simple expedient of saying, 'I don't love her
anymore; I love a younger woman'?" Then, in a quick leap
that obscures the fact that few men—except perhaps the
wealthiest—are compelled to support their "faithful wives" for
a moment longer than they are inclined to, she answers
sternly: "Even though love may go out the window, the obligation should remain. ERA would eliminate that obligation."

Feminists, too, addressed the situation of the financially dependent housewife, but it was the antifeminists who played on
her sense of vulnerability. While the feminist analysis spoke to
the housewife's anger and frustration, the antifeminist analysis
spoke to her fear—fear that she might, after all, be a parasite

whose support rested on neither love nor accomplishment, but only "obligation." At bottom, the antifeminists accepted the most cynical masculine assessment of the heterosexual bond: that men are at best half-hearted participants in marriage and women are lucky to get them.

In 1977 Phyllis Schlafly spelled out women's tenuous position in an apparent non sequitur that might have been lifted from *Playboy*'s early bulletins on the battle between the sexes. As Jane O'Reilly reports:

> She insisted that ERA would say: "Boys, supporting your wives isn't your responsibility anymore, and then they would no longer see it as their duty." Then she added: "Most wives spend all their husbands' money. He's lucky if he has anything left over when she gets through spending their money."[6]

A similar but more tactfully phrased assessment of the housewife's contribution appears in *The Power of the Positive Woman:*

> Household duties have been reduced to only a few hours a day, leaving the American woman with plenty of time to moonlight in full- or part-time jobs, or to indulge to her heart's content in a wide variety of interesting educational or cultural or homemaking activities.[7]

As William Iversen had argued in his classic *Playboy* article, "Death of the Hubby Image," no sane woman would abandon an occupation like this, and no sane man would voluntarily finance it.

Historical Perspective: On Booze and Ballots

The decade of the 1970s is not the first time that American women have rallied and organized against the threat of male irresponsibility. There was a similar movement in the late nineteenth century, which, like today's anti-ERA and anti-abortion movements, drew on a constituency of middle-class house-wives. This was the temperance movement, which at its peak mobilized nearly 200,000 women into the Women's Christian Temperance Union's campaign to close saloons and outlaw all "ardent spirits." According to historian Barbara Epstein, few of the women who became temperance crusaders were in a posi-tion—socially or economically—to have had direct contact with the disruptive effects of drink; alcohol was a symbolic issue, like abortion or ERA, a vivid reminder of women's vul-nerability within marriage. Epstein writes:

> In nineteenth-century America women—in some ways women of the middle strata specifically—were quite de-pendent upon marriage. Few women could find any alter-native to it that would bring any degree of material or emotional security—or respectability. . . . This meant that women's dependence upon men, their vulnerability to men, was extreme. The man that a woman married at twenty might turn out to be kind, responsible, and finan-cially successful; or he might turn out to be a drunken brute and a failure at business. Talking about temperance was a way of talking about these issues without attacking men (temperance literature always blamed the alcohol, not the man) and without criticizing the structure of the family (which was much too dangerous—or simply unthink-able—at a time when for the vast majority of women, there was no realistic alternative).[8]

Like today's pro-family crusaders, the temperance activists saw themselves protecting "Christian values" and the sanctity of the home, as well, of course, as the security of women. The difference—and it is a decisive one—is that when women orga-nized to protect their status as wives in the nineteenth century they had no trouble making common cause with the feminist movement of their time. The late nineteenth-century suffrage movement was equally dedicated to "home values," including temperance, and proposed to use the vote only to extend such values into the untidy domain of civic life. Aside from favoring women's entry into professions which could be represented as extensions of motherhood (like social work), the mainstream suffrage movement did not question the division of the sexes into breadwinners and homemakers and took pains to demonstrate that the ballot would not compromise woman's ability to cook, sew or comfort her work-weary provider. So the temperance movement made common cause with the suffrage movement and vice versa, around a shared commitment to "Home Protection" and a perception that "whatever breaks down the home, hurts woman most, because she is most dependent upon home affections for her happiness."[9]

One hundred years later, feminism itself could be portrayed as one of those pernicious forces, replacing the demon rum, that "breaks down the home." Feminists have tended to see this as either a vicious distortion or a misperception based on the unfortunate overstatements of a radical minority. But in our time, it is mainstream feminism that has embraced the goal, symbolized by ERA, of financial independence for women. That goal was too radical for late nineteenth-century feminism, and it has proved to be too radical for an influential minority of women in our own time. For insofar as financial independence is a legitimate and honorable status for some women, financial dependence is—perhaps unfortunately—less honorable for other women. In a battle over largely voluntary matters (such as whether men should marry, remain married or share their earnings with their wives) cultural legitimacy *is* the paramount stake. By simply asserting women's right to enter the labor market on an equal footing with men, feminism undercut the dependent housewife's already tenuous "right" to be supported. If some women can "pull their own weight"—as a resentful husband or a female follower of Phyllis Schlafly might reason—then why shouldn't all of them?

So, in our time, the women who mobilized to "protect the family," the spiritual descendents of temperance activists, parted company with the granddaughters of the suffragists. Instead of there being one movement to represent women in a hostile and uncertain world, we have had two—the feminist movement and the antifeminist movement. It is as if, facing the age-old insecurity of the family wage system, women chose opposite strategies: either to get out (figuratively speaking) and fight for equality of income and opportunity, or to stay home and attempt to bind men more tightly to them. Ironically, by choosing independence, feminists could make common cause with the male rebels of our generation, while the antifeminists could represent themselves as women's true defenders against the male rebellion. From the vantage point of the antifeminists, the crime of feminism lay not in hating men, but in trusting them too well.

The Far-right Connection

But the twentieth-century clash over women's rights—and men's obligations—involves much more than a strategic disagreement among women over the issue of economic security. The women quoted above as antifeminist leaders are also ranking functionaries in America's New Right, for whom the issues of marriage and male responsibility share space on a list that includes such concerns as the need to "rearm" America, check the tyranny of big government and impose the values of seventeenth-century Puritanism on a sinfully errant mass culture. Onalee McGraw is a consultant to the right-wing Heritage Foundation, which is dedicated, among other things, to expanding U.S. military power, restricting social service spending and promoting nuclear power. Kathleen Teague is the executive director of the American Legislative Exchange Council, which is opposed to gun control, occupational health and safety regulations and the "abuses" of organized labor. Phyllis Schlafly, the most prominent antifeminist organizer and spokeswoman, has been an activist on the far right for at least two decades before it reemerged, with fresh aspirations for state power, as the New Right.

Phyllis Schlafly has been acquainted with both the politics of the far right and the problem of male unreliability since early childhood, when the Depression threw her father into long-term unemployment. Apparently unshaken by his own experience with the free enterprise system, her father devoted his time to unsuccessful inventions and right-wing fulminations against Roosevelt and the New Deal. Phyllis's mother, meanwhile, entered the labor market and managed, by dint of almost superhuman efforts, to keep the family in the lower middle class and keep Phyllis in an elite Catholic girls' school, where the themes of Christian anticommunism were further reinforced. From there, Phyllis went on to put herself through college, win a scholarship to a master's degree program at Radcliffe, and become briefly successful as a publicist for right-wing agencies and candidates. But, as she has told her biographer, Carol Felsenthal, she had no intention of following in her mother's footsteps and becoming—even voluntarily—a career woman.[10] When she met a man who combined the virtues of ultraconservative politics with an exemplary potential for breadwinning, she promptly married him. Like other housewives in the era of the feminine mystique, she threw her awesome energies into homemaking, raising six children, "all of whom," as the book jacket of *The Power of the Positive Woman* boasts, "she taught to read at home before they entered school."

But, aside from this unusual effort, Phyllis Schlafly was not one of those housewives who, as Betty Friedan observed, let homemaking "expand to fill the time available" and crowd out all youthful ambitions. Sheltered by Fred Schlafly's more than ample income and assisted by a part-time housekeeper, she developed a new career as a one-woman propagandist for far-right concerns, publishing (and in some cases self-publishing) eight books on the twin menace of the Soviet Union and its domestic dupes. Politically, she kept one foot in the right-wing of the Republican Party and the other in the nether world of paranoid, evangelical organizations which made up what was then known complacently as the "lunatic fringe" of American conservativism. She ran for Congress as a Republican and wrote a best-selling book (*A Choice Not an Echo*) endorsing Barry Goldwater as the Republican candidate in 1964. At the same time, she believed that the party had been taken over by a "small group of secret kingmakers using hidden persuaders and psychological warfare techniques" to advance the interests of "the Red Empire." If this sounds like a highly imaginative view of the Republican Party, it was by no means unique to Phyllis Schlafly. The John Birch Society, a semi-secret right-wing organization that gained a sizable rural and suburban middle-class following in the early 1960s, had consistently warned that the United States was already "50%–70% Communist-controlled."[11] Like Schlafly, the Birch Society saw evidence of Red manipulation in any statesman or politician whose military aspirations fell short of nuclear Armageddon. In 1960, for example, the society's founder and director, Robert Welch, made the surprising announcement that President Dwight D. Eisenhower was himself a Communist operative.[12]

Whether Schlafly was a dues-paying member of the John Birch Society—which was notorious not only for its attacks on Republican stalwarts but for its overt racism and anti-Semitism —remains unclear. In 1960 Robert Welch praised her in the society's *Bulletin* as "a very loyal member of the John Birch Society." Later she denied membership, but it is a matter of public record that the society promoted (and in some cases distributed) her books and that she, in turn, spoke at Birch-sponsored events. It was this affiliation that crippled Schlafly's career as a mainstream Republican, but which also, not entirely inadvertently, helped launch her as the nation's leading anti-feminist.

The details of the metamorphosis from Phyllis Schlafly the anti-Communist crusader to Phyllis Schlafly the antifeminist crusader are known only to her. One factor, no doubt, was her inability to establish herself as a credible mainstream political figure within the Republican Party. In 1967 she lost her campaign for the presidency of the National Federation of Republican Women in part because of her alleged association with the John Birch Society. Then in 1970 she was defeated in a Congressional race against a conservative Democrat, whom she accused, oddly, of voting for "building roads in Yugoslavia." Throughout these dispiriting years, according to journalist Lisa Cronin Wohl, Schlafly maintained at least a "cordial relationship" with the Birch Society.[13] In 1972, both the Birch Society and Schlafly's newsletter flagged the ERA—

which at the time was solidly backed by the Republican Party—
as a major new political target, and within a few months,
Phyllis Schlafly emerged as the leader of a national campaign to
stop the ERA.

The most obvious reason for this sudden surge of right-wing
interest in a feminist issue was that, by the early seventies, the
old issues were not selling as well as they once had. Charges of
communism in high places sounded quaint in an America that
had had its own highly visible and hardly conspiratorial New
Left. Détente was in progress, anticommunism was on the decline, and sheer opportunism would have impelled the right to
exploit the new issues arising from the social changes of the
sixties—school busing, affirmative action, abortion and equal
rights for women. For Schlafly, in addition, as her chronicler
Lisa Wohl suggests, the ERA presented an opportunity to
"enter the mainstream," that is, to gain national attention
around an issue that had no apparent connection to the tired
themes of far-right paranoia. Others on the pro-ERA side
made the same assessment of the right-wingers who were beginning to appear reborn as antifeminists. Pointing to the connection between anti-ERA activism and the far-right American
Independent Party (which ran George Wallace for President in
1968 and Birch-affiliated John Schmitz in 1972), Congress-
woman Martha Griffiths charged that the anti-ERA effort was
really "a means of building a right-wing political organization
among women."[14] But if this was opportunism, it was hardly
unprincipled: The major themes of the right-wing assault on
feminism were latent in far-right anti-Communist ideology before feminism reappeared as a political force in America. And
the argument that clinched the antifeminist effort—that women
had to defend themselves in the face of male revolt—had been
spelled out on the far right at a time when Phyllis Schlafly was
still preoccupied with the roads of Yugoslavia and the imagined leftist leanings of Henry Kissinger.

The right had of course always been committed to upholding
the trinity of "God, Family and Country" (the title of the
Birch Society's annual public rallies), with family defined as
the union of a strong and reliable male with a fecund and pa-

triotically self-sacrificing female. In the calculus of the right, flag and family have never been independent variables: A threat to one is a threat to the other. Communism would abolish the family, and conversely, any loosening of traditional sex roles would weaken our defenses against communism. So you did not have to believe in the natural inferiority of women, or in the necessity of their confinement to the high-tech purdah of American middle-class kitchens, to see that there was something menacing about feminism. When the far right first caught sight of the women's movement, they saw—predictably—red. It was obvious, for example, to Birch Society commentator Alan Stang that the feminists who demonstrated at the 1969 Miss America Pageant were Communists, not only because of their ties to the New Left (which were easy enough to uncover), but because of their sinister insistence on day care for children. This was a dead giveaway of the feminists' ulterior motive: the collectivization of society and the enslavement of everybody by a totalitarian Communist government.

> The simple, obvious point of course is that the conspirators aren't just trying to destroy the family. They are also trying to take control of American children, who would be the cannon fodder in the total dictatorship they are trying to impose.[15]

Another reason to oppose feminism on the grounds of anticommunism stemmed from the fear that any blurring of gender roles would weaken the already debilitated American military beyond repair. The Birch-affiliated monthly magazine, *American Opinion,* offered a stream of alarming bulletins on the morale and status of the United States armed forces. The Russian soldier was "stupid," but blessed with an ancestry that included the "Tartars" and Genghis Khan; "So you've got a genetic mixture of wild energy, fierce courage, and patient endurance. Tough man."[16] Compared to the Soviet hordes, the American GI's were dangerously flaccid, pictured in Vietnam in interracial embraces and with flowers in their helmets. Every trend had to be assessed for its possible effect on our fighting men, already sapped by dope, "go go girls" and treasonous sellouts at high levels. Thus, male homosexuality was both a symptom of the tragic "debility" of "White culture" and part of a conspiracy to sissify the last remnants of American military manhood. After all, an *American Opinion* writer observed cunningly, the Communists didn't tolerate homosexuality in *their* countries, did they? In a fictional encounter with a gay male activist, published in 1971, a Bircher lays it on the line:

> Look, Susie Q, . . . the Comrades are stringing you sickies along because you're doing their work. They encourage you because you are weakening the country with your nasty games, but if they ever take over, you'll be among the first to get it.

But, according to this right-wing satirist, the gays continue to insist on their right to join the armed forces ("What fun!") and finally—tiring of the argument—break into a chant of "Bring our dear, dear boys home from Vietnam!"[17]

Feminism, as represented by the ERA, would take the subversion of the military a step further by making it " 'illegal' . . . to recognize a distinction between men and women." In *American Opinion*'s first article on the ERA, Congressman John Schmitz appealed less to chivalry than to hard-headed military pragmatism: The reason for having a strong military was ultimately to protect "our women." (An earlier article on the Soviet armed forces had ended with the curious image of Russian soldiers invading the ladies' room of the Chase Manhattan Bank.) "After all," Schmitz argued, never for a moment doubting that the ERA would mean instant conscription of American women into combat duty:

> . . . defense of our women and girls is one of the most basic reasons why we men are prepared to fight in defense of our homeland. If we were willing to see them killed, mutilated, or captured because they are "equal," we might as well say, "come and get them!"

And, along with the other absurdities posed by the abolition of gender, having an army full of girls would make us appear to be "the most foolish country in the world."[18]

So it was well within the parameters of old-fashioned an-

ticommunist paranoia to see feminism as a threat to national
security, even without appealing to misogyny or the more chivalrous versions of male supremacism. What was more innova-
tive was to present feminism as a threat to *women,* and this argument—which established the basis for the anti-ERA fight—
was laid out in John Birch Society literature in 1970, two years
before the ERA became a national issue. The credit for this
innovation belongs to an unlikely source of political analysis,
novelist Taylor (née Janet) Caldwell, the author of such best
sellers as *Dear and Glorious Physician* and *Never Victorious,
Never Defeated.* Like Ayn Rand, she often used her novels to
pit strong individuals against monstrous bureaucratic conspir-
acies. In *The Devil's Advocate,* for example, a small band of
"Minute Men" wage guerilla warfare against America's Communist conquerors. And like Phyllis Schlafly, she was hardly
typical of the dependent housewives whose interests she claimed
to represent; in fact, she said she had nothing but envy for
them, though the emotion could easily have been confused with
contempt:

> I envy them as I never envied another human creature.
> They tell me, with simpers, how much they "envy" me,
> and "how much you have accomplished, famous and all,
> while I am just a housewife," and I hate their complacent
> guts. For not one of them would exchange her life for
> mine, "fame" or not. They were brought up to be tenderly
> dependent—and they reap the rewards now of that
> upbringing.[19]

The article was entitled "Women's Lib: They're Spoiling
Eve's Great Con," and except for a few lapses into humorless
anticommunism, there was nothing which would have dis-
qualified it as a light piece in a mid-fifties' issue of *Playboy.*
Caldwell starts from the feminist premise that women can do
anything men can do. After all, she establishes in a maudlin
summary of her own rags-to-riches career, *she* had. The trick
was to make men believe otherwise—that women are weak and
helpless—and this was "the biggest Con Game, and the most
ancient, which one section of humanity has ever imposed on

another, since Eve invented it." What the poor victims derived
from being conned was not clear, for, with the least stirring of
female independence "the boys would catch on *and demand
liberation for themselves.* Which is exactly the calamity these
rampant females in the 'Liberation Movement' are going to
precipitate" (her emphasis). Only the illusion of feminine helplessness kept men in their place, and the illusion, she feared,
was wearing thin:

> I fear that men are beginning to suspect that we women
> conned them through the centuries. I fear they are asking
> themselves—to women's terrible hurt—why they should
> support an able-bodied woman who can earn a good living
> too, and why should a man give his ex-wife alimony and
> child-support checks, when she is just as capable, if not
> more so, of rolling up her sleeves and getting on the 8:30
> bus of a morning for an arduous day in the factory or
> office?

As an ominous example, she cites "a prosperous young man in
New York, in his early thirties, who has a 'pad' in a pent-
house" and "belongs to a Key Club" where he cavorts with
"Playmates."

> It's high time, he told me, that women "stopped being par-
> asites" and worked to the day they dropped dead or re-
> tired, as men do, and not expect a man "to support them."

Strangely, Caldwell did not consider the destructive effect of
women like herself, who stood as counter-examples to the
myth of universal female dependence. (And in her case, went
so far as to expose the myth in print!) In listing the causes of
male disillusionment, she cites, first, communism: ". . . Men
whisper among themselves—I have heard—that women in
Russia are treated *exactly* as men, and are farm-laborers plow-
ing and seeding . . . bricklayers and steelworkers . . . and do
the heaviest of manual labor." Next, she indicts the medical
profession:

> The men listen to modern "Liberal" doctors who say—the
> cads—that women are much stronger and healthier than

men, have more stamina, can do much more prolonged work, can bear children with ease and nonchalance, are healthy as horses, and therefore should . . . "take their places in the world, man to man."

As a result of the encouragements proffered by Communists, feminists and physicians, "men . . . are licking their lips and, for the first time in history, are readying themselves to be exploiters in their turn . . ."

What could a woman do to protect herself in the face of imminent, if not ongoing, male rebellion? Caldwell offered the advice she had given her own (successfully married) daughters, which, if extremist compared to later antifeminist nostrums, is still revealing. "I had told them from the beginning," she wrote, that unless a woman is "powerfully . . . motivated" and "deeply gifted" (thus establishing the narrow loophole through which she herself had escaped domesticity) "she should refrain from going out into the market places with mediocre abilities." For, "once she has earned a paycheck . . . she is practically doomed." The woman who had proved her wage-earning ability would only attract "the weak sisters among the men, who subconsciously realized that here was a girl who would earn a living for them." For the woman whose premarital existence was tainted by the experience of paid employment, the only hope lay in persuading men that this lapse had only been "a stop-gap before marriage," and in swearing, "Never again to earn money outside the home . . . Never again to be independent. In short, she should play the Big Con Game with her husband as shrewd and intelligent women have done for centuries."

The woman who can foreswear wage-earning as if it were a nasty habit, or the housewife of Phyllis Schlafly's imagination, who devotes most of her day to "educational and cultural activities," is obviously in an economic minority group. Over 20 percent of employed women are married to men who earn under $13,000 a year, and while a few of these underachieving husbands may be the "weak sisters" Caldwell warned about, it seems likely that the majority of them are hard-working, blue-collar men. In addition 24 percent of the American women who threaten the "con game" by resorting to the work force have no husbands at all, and an increasing number of these have small children of their own to support. Thus, the right's appeal to women, like its appeal to men, is class specific: directed to the woman who is a member of the middle or upper-middle class and whose membership depends on a contractual relationship with a man of that class. For the affluent male (and, indirectly, his wife) the right had always offered a program of economic self-interest: lower taxes, fewer regulatory obstacles to the predatory conduct of business, measures to restrict the perceived tyranny of labor, etc. The inspiration that helped transform the "old right," as represented by the John Birch Society, to the "New Right," as represented by Schlafly's STOP-ERA and a host of single-issue organizations with "pro-family" sympathies, lay in the realization that it was possible to appeal *directly* to affluent, but dependent women. The feminist movement, which looked from the right like a vast mobilization of women on the left, provided an example of what women could do as a political force. And the male revolt, which feminism brought into sharp focus, provided the anxiety around which to mobilize. For the affluent man, the right offered a way to hold on to his class privileges in the face of encroaching Communists, criminals, workers, etc. For the affluent woman, the right offered a way to hold on to a man.

The Right-wing Psychology of Men

Short of a program to indenture men into wage-earning for individual women, all that the right can actually offer is the restoration of a moral climate in which male rebellion will once more be either deviant, sinful or medically unwise. Part of this effort lies in the right's campaign to restore "the consequences" of heterosexual sex, by eliminating abortion and possibly contraception. Another part is the campaign to eliminate or criminalize homosexuality (and in the hate literature I have seen, the gays are disproportionately male). Then there are the multi-pronged efforts, often focused on the content and funding of education, which aim to popularize the Old Testament as a guide to everyday social relationships. Finally, and with less fanfare, there has emerged a New Right understanding of the psychology of men, a set of insights and assumptions which, once again, rationalizes conformity as a means to health.

Compared to the earlier conformist psychology represented by the neo-Freudians in the fifties and sixties, the New Right psychology is marked, above all, by a profound contempt for men. In the neo-Freudian scheme, men achieved maturity and mental health through their own efforts. They performed their "developmental tasks," at least most men did, and only the minority who fumbled at this undertaking were cordoned off for psychiatric attention as potential homosexuals or victims of permanent immaturity. In lay terms, the deviant minority were failures, half-men, weaklings. But in today's New Right ideology, *all* men are weak, and there is no redemption through individual works, or even "tasks." Men, in their weakness, are maintained in working order only by the constant efforts, demands and attentions of their wives.

Ann Patterson, an Oklahoma anti-ERA activist interviewed by Jane O'Reilly, put it this way:

> If you take away a man's responsibility to provide for his wife and children, you've taken away everything he has. A woman, after all, can do everything a man can do. *And* have babies. A man has awe for a woman. Men have more fragile egos.[20]

Here the paycheck has become instrumental to some larger therapeutic project, a psychodrama of family dependencies aimed at propping up the fragile male ego. All will be lost if a man's tenuous sense of self-esteem is challenged by a female paycheck, even a meager one. As Kathleen Teague of Virginia STOP-ERA and the American Legislative Exchange Council explained to me:

> If a man doesn't feel needed by his wife, he'll go out and find another woman who does need him. Take the case of a woman who's been a housewife, then she gets women-

libberized and goes into the work force. No matter what, her husband isn't going to feel he's number one in her life anymore. So she will lose him to a more conservative woman.

What a more conservative woman will offer is explained by Phyllis Schlafly in *The Power of the Positive Woman*. "A wife must appreciate and admire her husband," for the marriage will not last unless "she is willing to give him the appreciation and admiration his manhood craves."[21] Fortunately, women themselves have no such cravings, for she tells us, "Whereas a woman's chief emotional need is active (i.e., to love), a man's prime emotional need is passive (i.e., to be appreciated or admired)."

This new, 1970s style right-wing analysis of the heterosexual bond is a far cry from the traditional conservative view, in which the sexes were united by the natural, God-given, complementarity of male strength and female weakness. In the nineteenth century, for example, a common argument against women's suffrage was that women should not be allowed to vote for laws that they were physically incapable of enforcing, though, of course, no corpulent state legislator was ever called upon to apprehend and personally detain a lawbreaker. (Women's strength was presumed to be of an ethereal, moral kind, which would be instantly compromised by contact with a ballot box.) But today's New Right ideology inverts the traditional imagery of gender roles: Men are "passive, fragile"; while women are "active" and "can do everything." Taylor Caldwell's insistence on women's innate strength and competence is echoed again and again by Phyllis Schlafly. At the victory party for the defeat of the ERA, Schlafly attributed her side's victory to their greater self-confidence *as women*. The feminists, she said, "are victims of their own ideology; they believe that women can't do anything, that women are oppressed. But we of course know we . . . can go right out and do anything we want."

In their shift away from the traditional axis of male strength and activity vs. female weakness and passivity, our modern antifeminists were no doubt influenced by their own adversaries: feminism, with its insistence on women's strength and ability, and humanistic psychology, with its discovery of men's softness and vulnerability. For example, Tim LaHaye, a member of the national board of the Moral Majority and a prolific family-life advisor whose almost exclusive published source of information is the Bible, opens his 1977 book, *Understanding the Male Temperament,* on a note lifted from the literature of men's liberation:

> For the past thirty years, six-foot-four John Wayne has stalked through the American imagination as the embodiment of manhood. . . . He has left not only a trail of broken hearts and jaws everywhere, but millions of fractured male egos which could never quite measure up to the two-fisted, ramrod-backed character who conquered the Old West. The truth of the matter is that no man could measure up to that myth in real life—not even John Wayne.[22]

The revision of right-wing psychology that took men from being natural protectors to being natural weaklings has not been easy and is certainly not complete. After allowing men to dismount from the John Wayne image, LaHaye moves quickly to exonerate his fellows:

> Personally, I'm convinced that most men of our generation are as good as men have ever been. Oh, I have to admit that we hear regular reports of cop-outs, dissenters, and deserters of wives, children, and country today—but what's new about that? Western history reveals that we have always had "yellow-bellied hoss thieves" and wifebeaters.

The Heritage Foundation's Onalee McGraw seemed more conflicted by the contradictions between male behavior and what was formerly taken to be natural or divine law. At the beginning of our conversation she shared with me her "premise" that "the permanent heterosexual union is natural; I even say this is a quality given by a divine person and is written so to speak in the heart of man." Yet as she warmed to the subject of the male rebellion and the collapse of sanctions against footloose breadwinners, she asserted knowingly, "The men are going to leave [their wives] if they don't have to pay, because men are *this way*. Especially, you know, when they get into middle age."

Once it is admitted that what is "written on the heart of man" may be of the same genre as what is written on the walls of men's rooms, then the world becomes a much less secure place in which to marry and raise a family. As Schlafly's troops forthrightly admit, the interests of men no longer coincide with those of women, at least in the short term, and the short term may last until the onset of baldness and angina. Taken just a little further, the right's negative reappraisal of male nature implies that men are not just a problem for women, but for any kind of stable social order. This radical view, anticipated in rough outline by Freud, is the cornerstone of the social theory of the best-selling right-wing writer George Gilder. Gilder elevates the grasping anxiety of the Schlaflyites to a moral crusade: Men are *the* problem, and wives, in the old-fashioned sense, are the solution.

Gilder's Sexual Savagery

Perhaps it took a man to say it first. If a woman, even with right-wing credentials, had launched Gilder's extremist view of male psychology, she might have been accused of being a covert and vengeful female chauvinist, a man-hater, even, perhaps, a lesbian. Gilder is manifestly none of these. An intellectual among American New Rightists, he has taught at Harvard and published in high-brow magazines that rank-and-file members of the antifeminist right would repudiate as organs of Godlessness and moral relativism. Unlike other luminaries of the New Right, he entered Republican politics from the moderate edge of the spectrum, and has, by his own admission, befriended feminists and absorbed the literature of the human potential movement. His specific contribution has been to give the antifeminist suspicions about male nature a seemingly rational and scientific foundation: Men are in fact brutes, and this stems from their violent, impulsive and "nearly unremitting" sexual drives. Female sexuality, on the other hand, is diffuse and undemanding, "affirmed monthly in menstruation . . . through pregnancy, childbirth, lactation, suckling, and long-term nurture."[23] Thus, men's drives tilt toward rape and pillage, while a woman's could presumably be satisfied by finding a child's lost sneaker and other acts of "long-term nurture."

Gilder's "biology" is nineteenth-century Victorian social theory, renovated as one of those abiding "truths" that is easily lost in the shuffle of historical change. Like the Victorian theorists who preceded him, Gilder quickly extrapolates from biology to social policy: "The crucial process of civilization is the subordination of male sexual impulses and psychology . . ."[24] and this, not surprisingly, is a task for women. If men's impulses are barbaric, women's gentle cycles of nurture and vaginal bleeding are wonderfully congruent with the "predictable, regular" tempo of "modern society." Women must tame men, they must teach them to march to the slower beat of female hormonal rhythms, which are fortunately right in tune with the rhythms of industrial society. This is an old prescription, but Gilder has upped the ante. The Victorians also assigned women the task of "civilizing" men; with Gilder, however, this task has become tantamount to a police function:

> Whether the society can socialize most of its males—integrate them into both the community and the economy . . . will decide whether government has to spend much of its time and energy in controlling men or whether the men will willingly contribute their labor and spirit to the larger society.[25]

The most efficient solution to the problem Gilder presents would be a female government backed by an Amazonian army, but this is not even momentarily considered. Like social workers with disturbed and unruly clients, women are to "treat" men on a one-to-one basis and they are to do it through the long-term therapeutic process of marriage. Marriage is not only a way to regulate men's spasmodic sexual urges, it is the means through which men as breadwinners are compelled to "contribute their labor" to the larger society. In the scheme Gilder laid out in his 1973 book *Sexual Suicide,* neither jobs nor marriage are ends in themselves; both are instrumental to the all-consuming task of the social control of men. In fact, the jobs men perform as breadwinners might as well be make-work; the real purpose is to keep men off the streets. Gilder calculates that the "real contribution" individual men make through their work "rarely exceeds the real damage they can do if their masculinity is not socialized or subjected to female patterns." As for women's employment, it can only be seen as a dangerous disincentive for men to work. Momentarily abandoning his laissez-faire economic principles, Gilder proposes that pay differentials between the sexes actually be encouraged or (the mechanism is unclear) imposed where they are not already informally operative.

There is a chance, of course, that not all women will be willing to devote themselves to the supervision of individual males, and this possibility arouses Gilder's own innate male brutishness: "A society of relatively wealthy and independent women," he all but snarls, "will be a society of sexually and economically predatory males. . . . If they cannot be providers, they have to resort to muscle and phallus."[26]

Gilder represents the right's best effort, so far, to reestablish secular sanctions against male nonconformity. Psychiatry and psychology had once found that the man who failed as a breadwinner or declined to become one was immature and potentially homosexual. Gilder has gone a step farther and pronounced him a criminal. "The single man in general," he tells us,

> is disposed to criminality, drugs and violence. He is irresponsible about his debts, alcoholic, accident prone, and venereally diseased. Unless he can marry, he is often destined to a Hobbsean life—solitary, poor, nasty, brutish, and short . . .[27]

Even marriage is not a final cure, for the recidivist male impulses—"to give up the job, the family, and pursue a life of immediate gratification"—will keep popping up, checked only by the legal constraints against desertion and disorderly conduct. As the anti-ERA forces argued, not only women, but the legal and penal systems are required to keep men in line.

Thus, in the right's vision of the world, the battle of the sexes calls for a permanent state of war: The interests of the sexes are irreconcilably opposed; the survival of women demands the subjugation of men; the most intimate relationships must be used as instruments of a larger coercive scheme. It is, of course, a fragile dystopia, this antifeminist and right-wing vision of society, for if men were half as vicious as the right believes, few women would consort with them. And if single men were all by nature "disposed to criminality, drugs and violence," no woman would marry one.

11

CONCLUSION
For Women, Surviving the Aftermath

This book can be read as a story of mounting perfidy. We began in a moral climate that honored, in men, responsibility, self-discipline and a protective commitment to women and children. We moved, chapter by chapter, toward a moral climate that endorsed irresponsibility, self-indulgence and an isolationist detachment from the claims of others—and endorsed these as middle-class virtues and even as signs of "health." Those who come to this story from the political right will no doubt find here new reason to believe in the destructive effects of "permissiveness." They will be confirmed in their distrust of a secular society in which the old bonds of obligation and authority no longer hold, and in which the most transient satisfactions become reasonable motives. In a similar spirit, many readers from the left will strengthen their case against consumer capitalism, with its endlessly renewable spectacle of temptations. Here they will have found fresh evidence that capitalism itself acts as a tidal force wearing away against the family, or against any of the human attachments that sustain us in an amoral world. Finally, readers from both the left and the right can take this as a part of that long story of the erosion of the American character that begins with David Riesman's *The Lonely Crowd* and continues in Christopher Lasch's *The Culture of Narcissism*. The male revolt, then, becomes one more symptom of mass neurosis and cultural atomization—only viewed, this time, by a woman whose subject is men rather than by a man whose subject is "man."

There is a more optimistic reading. If the male revolt has roots in a narcissistic consumer culture, it is equally rooted in the tradition of liberal humanism that inspires feminism. "Roles," after all, are not fit aspirations for adults, but the repetitive performances of people who have forgotten that it is only other people who write the scripts. Traditional masculinity, as the men's liberationists argue, is a particularly strenuous act, and as feminists have concluded, it is an act which is potentially hazardous even to bystanders. As the male revolt moved past paternalism (represented by the "good" husband and provider), and then past a kind of macho defiance (represented by *Playboy* and the Beats), it moved toward an androgynous goal that most feminists—or humanists—could only applaud. The possibility of honest communication between the sexes has been increased, so has the possibility that men may be willing to take on more of what have been women's traditional tasks . . . or so we may hope.

Finally, the male revolt can be seen as a blow against a system of social control that operates to make men unquestioning and obedient employees. If men are not strapped into the role of breadwinners, perhaps they will be less compliant as assemblers of nuclear weapons, producers of toxic wastes, or as white-collar operatives of the remote and unaccountable corporations that are, increasingly, our substitute for elected government. Thus, on the optimistic side, a case could be made for putting the male revolt in the long tradition of human efforts toward personal and collective liberation—in step with feminism and with some broad populist impulse toward democracy.

My own judgment, as the reader must know, is an ambivalent one. At times I have felt that the various trends and intellectual shifts examined here deserve to be called less a "revolt" than an accommodation. What had been understood as masculinity, with its implications of "hardness" and emotional distance, was at odds with the more "feminine" traits appropriate to a consumption-oriented society, traits such as self-indulgence, emotional lability and a "soft" receptivity to whatever is new and exciting. The common drift, from *Playboy* through the counterculture of the sixties and the psychological reevaluation of masculinity in the seventies, has been to legitimate a consumerist personality *for men*. If this movement has had a vision, it has usually been a commoditized one: liberation as cocktails and Picasso prints in a bachelor apartment, liberation as tie-dyed shirts and fine wine, or as $60 running shoes and Adidas shirts. And, if this movement has had a sustaining sense of indignation, it has more often been directed against women rather than against the corporate manipulators of tastes and dictators of the work routine. Even the most self-conscious and articulate male rebels, the men's liberation spokesmen of the seventies, offered no more uplifting a vision than a little more leisure and good times for men—made possible, of course, by the reduced dependency of women.

The Beats were an exception: They did reject the entire round of work and consumption; they did offer a vision of human adventure beside which the commodified wonders of an affluent society looked pale and pointless. Yet their adventure did not include women, except, perhaps as "experiences" that men might have. And in their vision, which found its way into the utopian hopes of the counterculture, the ideal of personal freedom shaded over into an almost vicious irresponsibility to the women who passed through their lives.

But however we judge the male revolt—whether we see it as a childish flight from responsibility, an accommodation to the consumer culture, or as a libertarian movement on the scale of more familiar struggles for social change—the consequences for women are the same. Women too have fought against the family wage system, for if it confined men to the breadwinning role, it relegated women either to domesticity or, on the average, low-paid employment. We can imagine, if we like, that there have been two parallel struggles against the system that bound men to their work and women to men: one waged by men, which I have called the male revolt, and one waged by women, which is the feminist movement. But if we do think in terms of two parallel struggles, then we are forced to acknowledge, as Deirdre English has written, that "men won their freedom first."[1] For the consumer leverage that men gained has not been shared by women, while the responsibilities that men gave up have come increasingly to rest with us.

The starkest indicator of the changed economic relations between the sexes is what sociologist Diana Pearce has termed the "feminization of poverty."[2] In 1980 two out of three adults who fit into the federal definition of poverty were women, and more than half the families defined as poor were maintained by single women. In the mid-sixties and until the mid-seventies, the number of poor adult males actually declined, while the number of poor women heading households swelled by 100,000 a year (now 150,000 a year), prompting the National Advisory Council on Economic Opportunity to observe that

> All other things being equal, if the proportion of the poor in female householder families were to continue to increase at the same rate as it did from 1967 to 1978, the poverty population would be composed solely of women and their children before the year 2000.[3]

The fastest-growing group among America's female poor are single mothers, raising and supporting children on their own. Many are among the second or third generation poor, habitués of what conservatives like George Gilder call the "welfare culture." But many are also new recruits to poverty, women who had been middle class until divorce—or desertion—severed their claim on a man's wage. They have been called the "hidden poor" of America's suburbs: often left with the house and furniture but with no means of subsistence other than welfare, minimum-wage level jobs and (if they are fortunate) a trickle of child-support payments. For single mothers living at the edge of subsistence, whether they are case-hardened "welfare mothers" or members of the suburban *nouvelles pauvres,* there is only one thing left of the family wage system: the fact that women, on the average, are paid less than a family (at current urban rents, less than a very *small* family) requires for a moderate standard of living.*

Moving up from poverty and into the mainstream families that are still approvingly described as "intact," it is also clear that the assumptions of the family wage system have come to outweigh the reality. The average male wage is now less than that required to support a family, certainly less than required to support a family with middle-class expectations of family vacation trips, college educations for the children, and late-model cars. There are simply fewer jobs around that pay enough to support more than one or two people. As Caroline Bird points out in *The Two-Paycheck Marriage,* the number of "illpaid, dead-end 'women's jobs' grew so much faster [in the seventies] than better-paid 'men's work' that by 1976 only 40 percent of the jobs in the country paid enough to support a family."[4] With the decline of the auto and related industries in the seventies, more and more high-paid "men's jobs" have vanished, perhaps for good. In the economy of the 1980s, the only way most households can collect a family wage is by adding up the wages of individual family members—husbands, wives and often grown children as well.

Thus, if men have defaulted on the pact represented by the family wage, so too have their corporate employers. Near the turn of the century, the family wage system represented a pact between the social classes as well as the sexes. To the working class, it seemed to offer dignity and a certain gentility. To far-seeing capitalists and middle-class reformers, it seemed to offer social stability: Men who were the sole support of their families could be counted on to be loyal, or at least, fearful employees. And for many decades the system worked, more or less. Labor militancy subsided after the upheavals of the thirties, or at least ceased to pose the threat of insurrection. More and more people entered the mainstream culture centered on the breadwinning husband and stay-at-home wife and devoted

* Women in the United States earn, on the average, just over $10,000 a year, and according to the Bureau of Labor Statistics, it takes $25,407 a year to maintain a family of four at an "intermediate" standard of living.

themselves to the consumption of better houses, cars and leisure activities. If it was a dull life, as the male dissidents of the fifties complained, it was also what passed for the "good life." Personal consumption helped fuel general prosperity, and the domestic order based on the working husband and consumer-wife seemed to be eternally stable and even "natural."

But from the perspective of the eighties, the family wage system is already beginning to look like an artifact of affluence, and no more inherently stable than the price of oil or the value of the dollar. For one thing, it seems clear that the family wage has become a less attractive investment to the men who control corporate wealth. Money that might have sustained individual workers as sole breadwinners has gone to other uses: to overseas investments, to six-figure incomes for the managerial elite, or it is simply chasing other money in a paper whirlwind of speculation. At the same time, key consumer goods industries have narrowed their target populations to the "up-scale" consumers whose incomes put them "over the buying point." From the marketing outlook of the eighties, it does not seem to matter whether every family has the income to maintain a moderate level of consumption; it matters only that *some* households have the income to consume at the level of gluttony: Not, perhaps, a color television in every home, but *some* homes with wall-size television screens, video games, home computers and central air-conditioning. This is not the place to comment on the stability of an economic system that depends on a narrowing base of consumption and devotes a diminishing share of its productive capacity to the manufacture of useful goods. Suffice it to say that, for the time being, American capitalism stumbles ahead as if it had no further use for the diffuse affluence represented by the family wage system.

New Right leaders of the "pro-family" movement are, I think, frankly confounded by the collapse of the family wage system. Either they do not fully grasp what has happened or they refuse to confront the contradiction between their conservative economic convictions and their nostalgia for the traditional family. Phyllis Schlafly, for example, gave as one reason for opposing the ERA the fact that it would prevent employers

from inquiring into the marital status and breadwinning obligations of prospective employees. The implication was that if employers had this information, they could scale the wages they
offered accordingly. Yet, of course, there is nothing to obligate
an employer to pay the father of six more than the father of
two, nor would such an obligation be consistent with the right-
wing vision of free enterprise. Along the same lines, Con-
naught Marshner, chairman of the far-right Pro-Family Coali-
tion, suggested, in an interview with me, that there ought to be
"a system of differential minimum wages" scaled so that heads
of households are automatically paid "enough to support a
family." When I pointed out that this plan would require a
massive downward redistribution of wealth, such as is ordinarily accomplished only by revolution, she looked momentarily perplexed.

But the lesson of the male revolt is that even if all men *were*
suddenly offered wages sufficient to support families, there
would be no guarantee of economic security for women. Short
of a program to conscript men into marriage and (in recalcitrant cases) have male earnings deposited directly to their
wives' accounts, women have no sure claim on the wages of
men. For women as a group, the future holds terrifying insecurity: We are increasingly dependent on our own resources, but
in a society and an economy that never intended to admit us as
independent persons, much less as breadwinners for others.
Nostalgia for a romanticized past in which men were men and
women were safely at home will not help. Even if we wanted
to return to the feminine mystique, to the tenuous protection of
the family wage system, there is no going back.

* * *

If public policy cannot restore the family wage and the
breadwinner ethic, then public policy can at least acknowledge
their demise. To do so would require, for a start, a public commitment to implementing some of the most elementary goals of
feminism. They have been listed before, more fully and elo-
quently than I could hope to do. They were outlined at the International Women's Year conference in Houston in 1977, and

then presented to an indifferent administration. They have been reiterated more insistently, at an endless variety of forums, since the victory of an actively hostile administration. Here I will only restate, very briefly, two points that are fundamental to a feminist economic program.

First, that women should have the opportunity and the right to earn living wages—in fact, "family wages"—for themselves and those they support. This means an end to the occupational segregation that locks 80 percent of women workers into low-paid "women's jobs." It also means greater financial recognition for those jobs that have come to be considered "women's work"—clerical work, sales, light assembly, service work. We need an end to all the forms of discrimination, subtle and otherwise, that have kept women out of men's higher-paid crafts and professions; and, if we should choose a "woman's job," like nursing or clerical work, our work should still be valued with pay equal to what men receive in occupations requiring comparable levels of skill and effort.

I should add at once that the goal of financial independence for women, however "elementary" in the sense of having broad feminist support, is more radical than it may once have appeared. It is clear in the eighties, if it was not in the more prosperous sixties, that anti-discriminatory measures such as the ERA are not enough to guarantee women's economic well-being. It will not help to break out of women's occupational ghetto if there are fewer and fewer well-paying jobs outside of it, and it is hard to insist on higher pay from employers who are already busily dis-investing, fleeing overseas or replacing human labor with robots and microcomputers. For women (as well as for a growing number of men) the achievement of a family wage will require both a major redistribution of wealth and an economy planned to generate well-paying, useful employment—in short, an economic approach that is considerably to the left of anything in the current realm of American political discourse.

Second, on the list of "elementary" goals, women need a variety of social supports before they are able to enter the labor market on an equal footing with men or when they are unable to enter it at all. The most obvious and desperately needed service, both for women who are married and joint breadwinners and for those who are sole breadwinners, is reliable, high-quality child care. Job-training programs are another necessity, if only because so many of us, in all social classes, were educated for dependency and never offered the skills that might sustain us through long stretches of financial independence, if not for a lifetime. Finally, we need to recognize that at least for the foreseeable future, many women will find themselves in situations where they cannot enter the labor market at all—either because they have small children to care for, or because they cannot yet find jobs that pay enough for material subsistence. This means an adequate program of government income support—something far more generous and dignified than our present system of welfare. It is worth recalling that, even before the present wave of budget cutbacks, there was no state where the combined benefits of Aid to Families with Dependent Children (the major form of public assistance) and food stamps was enough to bring a family *up to* the official poverty level.[5] For women supporting families on their own, unemployment means destitution, and employment—at the level of the minimum wage—is not much of an improvement.

Feminists have fought for and demanded expanded social services since the beginning of our movement in the sixties: from a time when such a program seemed reasonable and even inevitable to a time when any expansion of government spending—other than military—is viewed as subversive to economic stability. Yet I believe that we need to push this set of demands even further: The collapse of the family wage system demands nothing less than the creation of a welfare state; that is, a state committed to the welfare of its citizens and prepared to meet their needs—for financial assistance, medical care, education, child care, etc.—when they are unable to meet these needs themselves.

The most common objection—that we can no longer collectively afford such services—deserves, I think, only brief refutation. There are two obvious sources of revenue for social purposes: (1) Increased corporate income taxes (corporate taxes have been declining steadily as a share of federal revenue since the 1950s, while the burden of financing government activities has been shifted to individuals), and (2) Drastically reduced military expenditures: As more and more people are coming to realize, our present stock of missiles and counter-missiles does not constitute a "defense" for anyone, but a standing invitation to annihilation. The kind of defense program we most urgently need is a program of defense against the mounting *domestic* dangers of poverty, unemployment, disease and ignorance— that is, a welfare state.

If that phrase, "welfare state," has been made to sound morally distasteful by our current policy makers, we should recall that the family wage system was itself a kind of private-sector welfare system, in which a woman's only "entitlement" was her share of her husband's wage. Those who believe that it is somehow more honorable to rely on an individual man than on agencies created by public wealth are, I think, simply clinging to an idealized memory of male paternalism. The breadwinner ethic never had the strength of law or even the transient security of public policy. If men cannot be held responsible as individuals—and there is no way consistent with democracy to do so—then we must all become more responsible collectively.

There are those who will argue that a welfare state only substitutes one kind of paternalism for another. The conservative analysis of the social welfare programs of the sixties is that they failed, and that they failed because they engendered dependency and helplessness in their beneficiaries. (This, at least, is George Gilder's argument; others on the right argue that there is no further need for social welfare spending because the programs of the sixties *succeeded* so well.) I am more impressed by the analysis of scholars like Frances Fox Piven and Richard Cloward: that the social welfare programs introduced in the sixties—limited as they were—succeeded not only in lifting many of their direct beneficiaries out of poverty, but in enabling working people in the "near poor" (which includes so many women) to struggle for wage and benefit gains from their employers.[6] Not, as Pevin and Cloward would agree, that those programs are in any way adequate models for the future. In fact, one of the most important feminist criticisms of the programs designed by President Johnson's "Great Society" is that they tended to assume a society of male breadwinners and female dependents. Thus, for example, Aid to Families with Dependent Children, whose beneficiaries are single mothers and their children, has clung to the premise that the mere presence of a male in the household is a cure for poverty and a sufficient reason to suspend benefits. Job-training programs like CETA have been faulted for tracking women toward low-wage service employment and away from potentially well-paying technical skills. As Diana Pearce argues, social services need to be based on the "acknowledgement that more and more women are financially on their own; that the female headed household is here to stay."[7] Otherwise government programs end up perpetuating the myth of male paternalism and the reality of female financial dependence.

Nor is there any reason why social welfare programs have to be intrinsically paternalistic themselves. I will not recapitulate the arguments here, but Frank Riessman, Alan Gartner and many others have made a convincing case, over the past ten years, that publicly sponsored services do not have to be bureaucratically or professionally dominated, but can be actually generative of participatory citizenship and self-help initiatives.[8] Instead, for example, of Medicaid, which has served, among other things, as a bountiful subsidy to the medical profession and associated industries, government initiatives in health could be focused on the direct provision of care, on preventive measures and environmental improvement, and could be designed (as many successful but briefly funded programs have shown) to call forth active citizen involvement. And surely financial assistance does not have to bear the humiliating stigma associated with welfare: Consider the contrast between the administration of unemployment insurance, which is collected by both men and women, and welfare, which is primarily collected by women. There is no reason why an American welfare state could not work through institutions that are democratic, accountable, decentralized and respectful of individual dignity—and there is no reason why liberals and feminists should abandon this as a goal.

For my own part, I do not propose an expanded welfare state as an ultimate social goal, but as a pragmatic step that circumstances have finally forced upon us. My own utopian visions are far more socialistic, more democratic at every level of dialogue and decision-making, more "disorderly," as Paul Goodman would say, than anything that would ordinarily be described as a "welfare state." Yet we have very little immediate alternative. If women had won equality and economic independence before the collapse of the family wage system, we might be able to step right into the liberal feminist vision of an androgynous and fully capitalist society. But the collapse of the family wage system came first, before either the economy or the culture was ready to admit the *female* breadwinner on equal terms. The result is that, for an increasing number of women and children, the services that might comprise an adequate welfare state have become a matter of survival.

* * *

But, finally, what about the men? For there is, of course, more at stake here than their wages. The collapse of the breadwinner ethic, and with it, the notion of long-term emotional responsibility toward women, affects not only the homemaker who could be cut loose into poverty, but the financially self-sufficient working woman, not to mention the children of either. For better or for worse, most of us grew up expecting that our lives would be shared with those of the men in our generation; that we would be married, or as we later put it in the modern vernacular, that we would have "long-term committed relationships." Only within those relationships could we imagine having children (and not only because of the financial consequences of motherhood) or finding the emotional support to do what we increasingly identified as *our* own things. Yet we—and the "we" here includes many more than feminists, professional women and others that conservatives might dismiss as marginal groups—face the prospect of briefer "relationships," punctuated by emotional dislocations and seldom offering the kind of loyalty that might extend into middle age. If we accept the male revolt as a historical fait accompli, and begin to act on its economic consequences for women—which is what I have argued that we must do—are we not in some way giving up on men, much as the right has already done? Are we acquiescing to a future in which men will always be transients in the lives of women, and never fully members of the human family?

To an extent, this is what women are beginning to do: looking for emotional support and loyalty from other women, while remaining, in most cases, sexually inclined toward men. A neighbor, abandoned by her husband two years ago, still hopes to meet "a nice, reliable guy," but her daily needs for intimacy and companionship are met by a local women's support group. An acquaintance, single and successful in her own career, plans to have a baby on her own with the support of women friends who are committed to help out as "co-parents." Two divorced women in their fifties decide that it will be both cheaper and less lonely to share the suburban house that one of them inherited from her marriage. According to Howard University professor Harriet McAdoo, there has always been a strong tradition of mutual support among urban black women, and a similar pattern is now beginning to emerge among the growing number of single women in the suburbs. It may mean practical help, like the exchange of baby-sitting or the loan of a credit card, and it usually means affectionate support— friends to call in a moment of depression or to share a holiday meal with. These are small steps, improvisations, but they grow out of a clear-headed recognition that there is no male bread-winner to lean on—and probably not much use in waiting for one to appear.

Yet I would like to think that a reconciliation between the sexes is still possible. In fact, as long as we have sons as well as daughters, it will have to happen. "Grown-up," in the case of men, should have some meaning for a boy other than "gone away"; and adulthood should mean something more than moral vagrancy. If we cannot have—and do not want—a binding pact between the sexes, we must still have one between the generations, and that means there must be some renewal of loyalty and trust between adult men and women. But what would be the terms of such a reconciliation? We have seen the instability—and the indignity—of the bond based on a man's earnings and woman's dependence. We cannot go back to a world where maturity meant "settling," often in stifled desperation, for a life perceived as a "role." Nor can we accept the nightmare anomie of the pop psychologists' vision: a world where other people are objects of consumption, or the chance encounters of a "self" propelled by impulse alone.

I can see no other ethical basis for a reconciliation than the feminist principle—so often repeated—that women are also persons, with the same needs for respect, for satisfying work, for love and pleasure—as men. As it is, male culture seems to have abandoned the breadwinner role without overcoming the sexist attitudes that role has perpetuated: on the one hand, the expectation of female nurturance and submissive service as a matter of right; on the other hand, a misogynist contempt for women as "parasites" and entrappers of men. In a "world without a father," that is, without the private system of paternalism built into the family wage system, we will have to learn to be brothers and sisters.

Then, finally I would hope that we might meet as rebels together—not against each other but against a social order that condemns so many of us to meaningless or degrading work in return for a glimpse of commodified pleasures, and condemns all of us to the prospect of mass annihilation. If we can do this, if we can make a common commitment to ourselves and future generations, then it may also be possible to rebuild the notion of *personal* commitment, and to give new strength and shared meaning to the words we have lost—responsibility, maturity and even, perhaps, manliness.

NOTES

Chapter 1: Introduction

1. Nicholas David, "Courtship on the Campus," *Esquire*, February 1958, p. 48.
2. Louise Kapp Howe (ed.), *The Future of the Family* (New York: Simon & Schuster, Inc., 1972), p. 21.
3. Arthur Calhoun, *Social History of the American Family, Vol. III; Since the Civil War* (Cleveland: The Arthur H. Clark Co., 1919), p. 160.
4. Charlotte Perkins Gilman, *Women and Economics*, Carl N. Degler (ed.), (New York: Harper Torchbooks, 1966), p. 22.
5. H. L. Mencken, *In Defense of Women* (New York: Alfred A. Knopf, Inc., 1918), p. 122.
6. Heidi Hartmann, "The Unhappy Marriage of Marxism and Feminism: Towards a More Progressive Union," in Lydia Sargent (ed.), *Women and Revolution* (Boston: South End Press, 1981), p. 1.
7. Barbara Ehrenreich and Deirdre English, *For Her Own Good: 150 Years of the Experts' Advice to Women* (Garden City, N.Y.: Anchor Press/Doubleday, 1978).
8. Carol Brown, "Mothers, Fathers, and Children: From Private to Public Patriarchy," in Sargent, op. cit., p. 245.
9. Theodore Roosevelt, Address to the First International Congress on the Welfare of the Child, Washington, D.C., March 1908.
10. Jessie Bernard, *The Future of Marriage* (New York: World Publishing, 1972), p. 18.
11. Lenore J. Weitzman, *The Marriage Contract: Spouses, Lovers, and the Law* (New York: The Free Press, 1981), pp. 40–41.
12. National Advisory Council on Economic Opportunity, *Final*

Report: The American Promise, Equal Justice and Economic Opportunity (Washington, D.C.: U. S. Government Printing Office, 1981), p. 13.

Chapter 2: Breadwinners and Losers

1. Dr. Hendrik M. Ruitenbeek, *Psychoanalysis and Male Sexuality* (New Haven: College and University Press, 1966), p. 12.
2. Therese Benedek, "Fatherhood and Providing," in E. James Anthony and Therese Benedek (eds.), *Parenthood: Its Psychology and Psychopathology* (Boston: Little, Brown & Co., 1970), p. 167.
3. A. Alvarez, "Repenting at Leisure in the 1950s," *Atlantic,* March 1982, p. 34.
4. H. A. Overstreet, *The Mature Mind* (New York: W. W. Norton & Co., Inc., 1950).
5. Elizabeth B. Hurlock, *Developmental Psychology* (New York: McGraw-Hill Int. Bk. Co., 1975, first published 1959), p. 209.
6. Stella R. Goldberg and Francine Deutsch, *Life-Span, Individual and Family Development* (Monterey, Calif.: Brooks/Cole Publishing Co., 1977), p. 250.
7. Justin Pikunus, *Human Development: A Science of Growth* (New York: McGraw-Hill Int. Bk. Co., 1969), p. 333.
8. Dorothy Walter Baruch, Ph.D., and Hyman Miller, M.D., *Sex in Marriage* (New York: Hart Publishing Co., 1962), p. 12.
9. Philip Roth, *When She Was Good* (New York: Random House, 1966), p. 218.
10. Talcott Parsons, "Age and Sex in the Social Structure of the United States," in Clyde Kluckhohn and Henry A. Murray (eds.), *Personality in Nature, Society and Culture* (New York: Alfred A. Knopf, Inc., 1949), p. 273.
11. Henry C. Lindgren, *Psychology of Personal and Social Adjustment* (New York: American Book Co., 1959), p. 479.
12. Manfred Kuhn, "How Mates Are Sorted," in Howard Becker and Reuben Hill (eds.), *Family, Marriage and Parenthood* (Boston: Health Books, 1955).
13. Paul Popenoe, "Mate Selection," in Judson T. and Mary Glandis (eds.), *Building a Successful Marriage* (Englewood Cliffs, N.J.: Prentice-Hall, Inc., 1968), p. 48.

14. Richard Burnett, M.D., "Adulthood," in George H. Wiederman, M.D. and Sumner Matison (eds.), *Personality Development and Deviation: A Textbook for Social Work* (New York:
International Universities Press, 1975), p. 24.

15. William H. Wainwright, M.D., "Fatherhood as a Precipient of
Mental Illness," *American Journal of Psychiatry*, Vol. 123, No.
1, July 1966, p. 40.

16. Lucie Jessner, Edith Weigert and James L. Foy, "The Development of Parental Attitudes During Pregnancy," in Wiederman
and Matison, op. cit., p. 214.

17. Hendrik M. Ruitenbeek, "Men Alone: The Male Homosexual
and the Disintegrated Family," *The Problem of Homosexuality
in Modern Society* (New York: E. P. Dutton, Inc., 1963),
p. 80.

18. Kenneth S. Lynn, "Adulthood in American Literature," in Erik
Erikson (ed.), *Adulthood* (New York: W. W. Norton & Co.,
Inc., 1976), p. 237.

19. Abram Kardiner, "The Flight from Masculinity" in Hendrik
M. Ruitenbeek (ed.), *The Problem of Homosexuality in Modern America* (New York: E. P. Dutton, Inc., 1963), p. 27.

20. Lionel Ovesey, M.D., *Homosexuality and Pseudohomosexuality* (New York: Science House, 1969), pp. 24–25.

21. Ibid., p. 137.

22. Ibid., pp. 139–40.

23. Roth, op. cit., p. 293.

24. Herman Wouk, *Marjorie Morningstar* (Garden City, N.Y.:
Doubleday & Company, Inc., 1955), p. 530.

Chapter 3: Early Rebels

1. Robert Lindner, *Must You Conform?* (New York: Rinehart
Co., 1955), p. 23.

2. Daniel Bell, *The End of Ideology* (New York: The Free Press,
1960), p. 35.

3. George B. Leonard, Jr., "The American Male: Why Is He
Afraid to Be Different?" *Look*, February 18, 1958, p. 95.

4. Richard Yates, *Revolutionary Road* (Boston: Little, Brown &
Co., 1961), pp. 65–66.

5. Ibid., p. 129.
6. David Riesman, *The Lonely Crowd* (New Haven: Yale University Press, 1950), p. 21.
7. Ibid., p. 18.
8. Ibid., p. 41.
9. Ibid., p. 127.
10. Alan Harrington, "Life in the Crystal Palace," in Eric and Mary Josephson (eds.), *Man Alone: Alienation in Modern Society* (New York: Dell Publishing Co., Inc., 1962), pp. 133–43.
11. Bell, op. cit., p. 48.
12. Riesman, op. cit., p. 220.
13. Stewart H. Holbrook, "The Vanishing American Male," *American Mercury*, March 1937, p. 270.
14. Philip Wylie, "The Abdicating Male . . . and How the Gray Flannel Mind Exploits Him Through His Women," *Playboy*, November 1956, p. 29.
15. J. Robert Moskin, "The American Male: Why Do Women Dominate Him?" *Look*, February 4, 1958, p. 77.
16. Wylie, loc. cit.
17. Moskin, loc. cit.
18. William Atwood, "The American Male: Why Does He Work So Hard?" *Look*, March 4, 1958, p. 71.
19. Yates, op. cit., pp. 111–12.
20. Riesman, op. cit., p. 243.
21. Norman Podhoretz, *Doings and Undoings: The Fifties and After in American Writing* (New York: Farrar, Straus & Co., Inc., 1964), p. 109.

Chapter 4: Playboy Joins the Battle of the Sexes

1. Quoted in Joe L. Dubbert, *A Man's Place: Masculinity in Transition* (Englewood Cliffs, N.J.: Prentice-Hall, Inc., 1979), p. 269.
2. "Meet the *Playboy* Reader," *Playboy*, April 1958, p. 63.
3. Hugh Hefner, "The Playboy Philosophy," *Playboy*, January 1963, p. 41.

4. Frank Brady, *Hefner* (New York: Macmillan Pub. Co., Inc., 1974), p. 98.

5. Quoted in Douglas T. Miller and Marion Nowak, *The Fifties* (Garden City, N.Y.: Doubleday & Company, Inc., 1977), p. 119.

6. Phil Silvers, "Resolution: Never Get Married," *Playboy*, January 1957, p. 77.

7. Burt Zollo, "Open Season on Bachelors," *Playboy*, June 1953, p. 37.

8. Quoted in Myron Brenton, *The American Male* (New York: Coward, McCann, 1966), p. 30.

9. Zollo, loc. cit.

10. William Iversen, "Love, Death and the Hubby Image," *Playboy*, September 1963, p. 92.

11. "Think Clean," *Time*, March 3, 1967, p. 76.

Chapter 5: The Beat Rebellion

1. Jack Kerouac, *The Dharma Bums* (New York: Viking Press, Inc., 1958), p. 77.

2. Paul O'Neil, "The Only Rebellion Around," *Life*, November 30, 1959, p. 114.

3. Gene Feldman and Max Gartenberg, *The Beat Generation and the Angry Young Men* (New York: Citadel Press, 1958), p. 12.

4. Jack Kerouac, *On the Road* (New York: New American Library, 1957), pp. 159–60.

5. Ibid., p. 161.

6. Ibid., p. 9.

7. John Clellon Holmes, "The Philosophy of the Beat Generation," *Esquire*, February 1958, p. 35.

8. Norman Podhoretz, *Doings and Undoings: The Fifties and After in American Writing* (New York: Farrar, Straus & Co., Inc., 1964), p. 157.

9. "Squaresville, U.S.A. vs. Beatsville," *Life*, September 21, 1959, p. 31.

10. Francis J. Rigney and L. Douglas Smith, *The Real Bohemia* (New York: Basic Books, 1961).

Chapter 6: Reasons of the Heart

1. Quoted in G. Stanley Hall, *Adolescence,* Vol. II (New York: D. Appleton, 1905), p. 588.
2. Ingrid Waldron, "Why Do Women Live Longer than Men?" *Social Science and Medicine,* Vol. 10, 1976, p. 349.
3. Lemuel C. McGel, M.D., "The Suicidal Cult of Manliness," *Today's Health,* January 1957, p. 28.
4. Ashley Montagu, *The Natural Superiority of Women* (New York: Collier Books, 1952), p. 79.
5. Aaron Antonovsky, "Social Class and the Major Cardiovascular Diseases," *Journal of Chronic Diseases,* Vol. 21, 1968, p. 65.
6. Fred Kerner, *Stress and Your Heart* (New York: Hawthorn Books, 1961), p. 167.
7. Alice Lake, "Five Husbands Who Might Have Lived," *McCall's,* November 1964, p. 126.
8. Arthur Blumenfeld, *Heart Attack: Are You a Candidate?* (New York: Paul S. Eriksson, 1964), p. 7.
9. John Kenneth Galbraith, *The Affluent Society* (Boston: Houghton Mifflin Co., 1958), p. 253.
10. Robert Wallace, "A Stricken Man and His Heart," *Life,* May 9, 1955, p. 143.
11. Kerner, op. cit., p. 66.
12. Ibid., pp. 22–23.
13. Ibid., pp. 76–77.
14. Quoted in *U.S. News and World Report,* March 21, 1977, p. 51.
15. Suzanne Haynes and Manning Feinleib, "Women, Work and Coronary Heart Disease," *American Journal of Public Health,* Vol. 70, 1980, p. 133. See also Barbara Ehrenreich, "Is Success Dangerous to Your Health: The Myths and Facts about Women and Stress," *Ms.,* May 1979, p. 51.
16. Allan Johnson, personal communication, 1979.
17. Howard Sprague, M.D., "Be Glad You're a Woman—You'll Live Longer," *Ladies' Home Journal,* November 1964, p. 43.
18. Daniel E. Schneider, *Psychoanalysis of Heart Attack* (New York: Dial Press, 1967), p. 207.

19. Ibid., pp. 148–49.
20. "They Ran the Heart Study," *Business Week*, December 12, 1964, p. 51.
21. C. D. Jenkins, "Psychological and Social Precursors of Coronary Disease," *New England Journal of Medicine*, Vol. 284, 1977, p. 244.
22. "Coronary Candidates," *Newsweek*, November 4, 1963, p. 63.
23. McGel, loc. cit.
24. "What You Can Do to Help Your Husband Avoid a Heart Attack," *Good Housekeeping*, April 1965, p. 180.
25. "Can I Help My Husband Avoid a Heart Attack?" *Reader's Digest*, September 1962, p. 69.
26. Marya Mannes in Harold H. Hart (ed.), *Marriage: For and Against* (New York: Hart Publishing Co., 1972), p. 34.

Chapter 7: From Conformity to "Growth"

1. Abraham H. Maslow, *Toward a Psychology of Being* (New York: Van Nostrand, 1968), p. 3.
2. Richard J. Lowry (ed.), *The Journals of A. H. Maslow*, Vol. I (Monterey, Calif.: Brooks/Cole Publishing Co., 1979), p. 113.
3. William C. Schutz, *Joy: Expanding Human Awareness* (New York: Grove Press, 1967), p. 15.
4. Joel Kovel, M.D., *A Complete Guide to Therapy* (New York: Pantheon Books, 1976), p. 166.
5. Russell Jacoby, *Social Amnesia: A Critique of Conformist Psychology from Adler to Laing* (Boston: Beacon Press, 1975), pp. 57–58.
6. Maslow, op. cit., p. 31.
7. Lowry, op. cit., p. 81.
8. Martin L. Gross, *The Psychological Society* (New York: Random House, 1978), p. 304.
9. Frederick Perls, Ralph Hefferline and Paul Goodman, *Gestalt Therapy: Excitement and Growth in the Human Personality* (New York: Delta, 1951), p. 298.
10. Ibid., p. 304.
11. George Bach and Herb Goldberg, *Creative Aggression: The Art of Assertive Living* (Garden City, N.Y.: Doubleday & Company, Inc., 1974), pp. 391–92.

12. David Viscott, M.D., *Feel Free* (New York: Dell Publishing Co., 1971), pp. 9–10.

13. Mel Krantzler, *Creative Divorce: A New Opportunity for Personal Growth* (New York: M. Evans & Co., 1973), pp. 235–36.

Chapter 8: The Androgynous Drift

1. Betty Friedan, *The Feminine Mystique* (New York: W. W. Norton & Co., Inc., 1963), pp. 255–56.

2. Ibid., pp. 271–72.

3. Fred J. Cook, *The Nightmare Decade* (New York: Random House, 1971), p. 6.

4. Mickey Spillane, *One Lonely Night* (New York: E. P. Dutton, Inc., 1951), p. 171.

5. Michael Herr, *Dispatches* (New York: Alfred A. Knopf, Inc., 1977), p. 16.

6. Marc Feigen Fasteau, *The Male Machine* (New York: McGraw-Hill Int. Bk. Co., 1974), p. 159.

7. Leonard Kriegel, *On Men and Manhood* (New York: Hawthorn Books, 1979), p. 35.

8. Jesse Kornbluth (ed.), *Notes from the New Underground* (New York: Viking Press, Inc., 1968), p. 38.

9. Quoted in Kornbluth, op. cit., p. 205.

10. Dennis McNally, *Desolate Angel: Jack Kerouac, the Beat Generation and America* (New York: McGraw-Hill Int. Bk. Co., 1979), p. 315.

11. Charles Reich, *The Sorcerer of Bolinas Reef* (New York: Random House, 1976), p. 77.

12. Ibid., p. 46.

13. Ibid., p. 47.

14. Ibid., p. 53.

15. Ibid., p. 140.

16. Charles Reich, *The Greening of America* (New York: Random House, 1970), p. 228–29.

17. Patricia Coffin, "A Message to the American Man," *Look*, January 10, 1967, p. 14.

18. Joe David Brown (ed.), *The Hippies* (New York: Time/Life Books, 1967), p. 13.
19. Gloria Steinem, "What It Would Be Like if Women Win," *Time*, August 31, 1970, p. 22.

Chapter 9: The Male Revolt Redeemed

1. Barry Farrell, "You've Come a Long Way, Buddy," *Life*, August 27, 1971, p. 51.
2. Warren Farrell, *The Liberated Man* (New York: Bantam Books, 1975), p. xxii.
3. Quoted in "Men's Movement Taking Off," *Newsday*, October 27, 1981, Part II, p. 7.
4. Herb Goldberg, Ph.D., *The Hazards of a Being Male: Surviving the Myth of Masculine Privilege* (New York: Signet, 1976), p. 162.
5. Joseph Veroff, Elizabeth Douvan and Richard A. Kulka, *The Inner American: A Self-Portrait from 1957 to 1976* (New York: Basic Books, 1981), p. 191.
6. Goldberg, op. cit., p. 170.
7. Andrew Hacker, "Farewell to the Family?" *New York Review of Books*, March 18, 1982, p. 37.
8. Linda Wolfe, "The Good News: The Latest Expert Word on What It Means to Be Single," *New York*, December 28, 1981–January 4, 1982, p. 33.
9. Quoted in Betty Friedan, *The Second Stage* (New York: Summit Books, 1981), p. 137.
10. Quoted in *Newsday*, loc. cit.
11. Marc Feigen Fasteau, *The Male Machine* (New York: McGraw-Hill Int. Bk. Co., 1974), p. 1.
12. Robert Brannon, "The Male Sex Role: Our Culture's Blueprint of Manhood, and What It's Done for Us Lately," in Deborah S. David and Robert Brannon (eds.), *The Forty-Nine Percent Majority* (Reading, Mass.: Addison Wesley, 1976), p. 4.
13. Ibid., p. 15.
14. Carol Ehrlich, "The Reluctant Patriarchs," in Jon Snodgrass (ed.), *For Men Against Sexism* (Albion, Calif.: Times Change Press, 1977).

15. Jack Sawyer, "On Male Liberation," *Liberation*, Vol. 15, 1970, p. 32.
16. Philip Rice, "On Being Male in America," *Voice*, Spring 1981, p. 1.
17. *Response*, January 1982, p. 13.
18. Quoted in *Swank*, February 1982, p. 57.
19. Goldberg, op. cit., pp. 190–91.
20. Dennis Altman, *The Homosexualization of America* (New York: St. Martin's Press, 1982), p. 6.
21. Quoted in Altman, op. cit., p. 42.
22. Richard G. Abell with Corlis Wilber Abell, *Own Your Own Life* (New York: Bantam Books, Inc., 1977), p. 10.
23. Ibid., p. 40.
24. Ibid., pp. 41–42.
25. Quoted in Warren Farrell, op. cit., p. 66.
26. Warren Farrell, op. cit., p. 41.
27. Joseph H. Pleck, "The Male Sex Role: Definitions, Problems and Sources of Change," *Journal of Social Issues*, Vol. 32, 1976, p. 155.
28. Andrew Tolson, *The Limits of Masculinity* (London: Tavistock, 1977), pp. 63–64.
29. Meyer Friedman, M.D. and Ray H. Rosenman, M.D., *Type A Behavior and Your Heart* (New York: Alfred A. Knopf, Inc., 1974).
30. Ibid., p. 191.
31. Ibid., p. 203.

Chapter 10: Backlash

1. Quoted in Jane O'Reilly, *The Girl I Left Behind* (New York: Macmillan Pub. Co., Inc., 1980), p. 189.
2. "Opposition Rises to Amendment on Equal Rights," New York *Times*, January 15, 1973, p. 1.
3. Randy Engel, "The Family Under Siege," *American Life Lobby*, Vol. 1, Fall 1980, p. 1.
4. Onalee McGraw, "The Family, Feminism, and the Therapeutic State," The Heritage Foundation (no date), p. 11.
5. Phyllis Schlafly, *The Power of the Positive Woman* (New Rochelle, N.Y.: Arlington House, Inc., 1977), p. 76.

6. O'Reilly, op. cit., p. 198.

7. Schlafly, op. cit., p. 5.

8. Barbara Epstein, "Woman's Temperance, Home Protection, and Proto-Feminism in Late Nineteenth-Century America," paper presented to the Organization of American Historians' annual meeting, 1981. See also Barbara Epstein, *The Politics of Domesticity* (New York: Columbia University Press, 1981).

9. Quoted in Epstein, "Woman's Temperance . . ."

10. Carol Felsenthal, *The Sweetheart of the Silent Majority* (Garden City, N.Y.: Doubleday & Company, Inc., 1981).

11. Quoted in Benjamin R. Epstein and Arnold Forster, *Danger on the Right* (New York: Random House, 1964), p. 12.

12. Ibid., pp. 40–41.

13. Lisa Cronin Wohl, "Phyllis Schlafly: The Sweetheart of the Silent Majority," *Ms.*, March 1974, p. 54.

14. New York *Times*, March 15, 1973, p. 21.

15. Alan Stang, "War on Women: They're Saying Miss America Is a Fascist," *American Opinion*, December 1969, p. 39.

16. Medford Evans, "The Red Army: Bulwark or Threat to Communism?" *American Opinion*, February 1971, p. 23.

17. John Brennan, "Gay Libb," *American Opinion*, March 1971, p. 37.

18. John G. Schmitz, "Look Out! They're Planning to Draft Your Daughter," *American Opinion*, November 1972, p. 1.

19. Taylor Caldwell, "Women's Lib: They're Spoiling Eve's Great Con," *American Opinion*, September 1970, p. 27.

20. Jane O'Reilly, "The Big-Time Players behind the Small-Town Image," *Ms.*, January 1983.

21. Schlafly, op. cit., pp. 54–55.

22. Tim LaHaye, *Understanding the Male Temperament* (Charlotte, N.C.: Commission Press, 1977), p. 11.

23. George Gilder, *Sexual Suicide* (New York: Quadrangle, 1973), p. 17.

24. Ibid., p. 23.

25. Ibid., p. 95.

26. Ibid., p. 97.

27. George Gilder, *Naked Nomads* (New York: Times Books, 1974), p. 10.

Chapter 11: Conclusion

1. Deirdre English, "The War Against Choice," *Mother Jones*, February/March 1981, p. 16.
2. Diana Pearce, "The Feminization of Poverty: Women, Work and Welfare," *Urban and Social Change Review*, February 1978, p. 28.
3. National Advisory Council on Economic Opportunity, *Final Report: The American Promise, Equal Justice and Economic Opportunity*, (Washington, D.C.: U. S. Government Printing Office, 1981), p. 46.
4. Caroline Bird, *The Two-Paycheck Marriage* (New York: Wade Rawson Pubs., Inc., 1979), p. 4.
5. *A Children's Defense Budget: A Response to Reagan's Black Book* (Washington, D.C.: The Children's Defense Fund, 1981), p. 6.
6. Frances F. Piven and Richard A. Cloward, *The New Class War*, (New York: Pantheon Books, Inc., 1982).
7. Diana Pearce, personal communication, 1982.
8. See, for example, Alan Gartner and Frank Riessman, *The Service Society and the Consumer Vanguard* (New York: Harper & Row, Pubs., 1974).

INDEX